The Ṛgveda in the Indus Inscriptions

Madhusudan Mishra
M.A., Ph.D. Diploma in Applied Linguistics

SHIPRA

ISBN: 81-7541-142-2

First Published in India in 2003

The Ṛgveda in the Indus Inscriptions

Published by :
SHIPRA PUBLICATIONS
115-A, Vikas Marg, Shakarpur,
Delhi-110092 (India)
Ph: 22458662, 22500954 Fax : 91-11-22458662
Email : siprapub@satyam.net.in
www.shiprapublications.com

Laser Typeset by:
Manas Enterprises
Delhi-110032

Printed at:
Chaudhary Offset Process,
Delhi-110051

बोद्धारो मत्सरग्रस्ताः प्रभवः स्मयदूषिताः।
अबोधोपहताश्चान्ये जीर्णमंगे सुभाषितम्।।

Those who know are envious. Those who have authority are arrogant. Others are reeling under ignorance: noble speech is languishing in mouth.

Contents

    1254 ma ṣa
    4225 ma ṇa
    4289 ra na ṣa
    4094 ṣa ra ṣa
    la rā ṭha
    ha dha bha
    The Vedic Sabda
    The text no. 8002:
    8050 ci ha ta ṭha
    4075 ci ha ra gha va ṇa ṣa
    riśādas
    ha ci. ha ca
    1267 la pa ma

Preface

With the supposition that it is my last work, I preface this book as a tired old man. Though my life has not been as pleasant as I wished it should have been, I am at least satisfied that I have discovered the most primitive form of the Aryan speech.

After a continuous engagement with the Indus inscriptions since April, 1994, I have been able to say that the Indus texts give specific messages in a genuine language. It has nothing to do with the words of the Nighaṇṭu, of the Dravidian etymological dictionaries, of the family-relationships, of the stars and planets, and so on. The seers of the Indus culture belong to a hoary past who had heard about the big bang, of the rolling golden egg, of the destruction caused by the avalanche of the glacial ages, which they have referred to in their little sentences. The Vedic seers have elaborated some of their ideas.

Any sign, graphically independent, often standing alone, does not impress anybody about its being a part of some genuine language. Even in Sanskrit, a sentence is defined as consisting of a verb, which also means the verb itself. Thus gacchati (he/she/it goes) is a complete sentence. In English also, just the order 'go' is not less than a clause. But when we see a single sign in the Indus seals, we refuse to agree that it is a clause. This blunt refusal on our part does not allow us to proceed on the decipherment of the Indus script.

The language is so antiquated that, even though it reflects

in its later phase, a whole clause reduced in form and mutilated semantically, rebukes any relationship of the two phases of the language. The expansion of the emaciated Vedic words to the Indus size is repugnant to the linguistic scholarship.

Even when the Vedic tánas (offspring) expanded to the Indus size ta na ṣa (from the womb gems come out) agrees in form and meaning and is remarkably identifiable, syllable by syllable, with the help of the syllabic order of the Māheśvara-sūtras, nobody is ready to offer any comment or to reject it with suitable arguments. This silence does not show any disagreement, but we are not perhaps ready to face the nacked truth. A veiled lie is, of course, acceptable, which has ruled almost for a century.

Some of the monosyllabic words of the inscriptions are still current in our society. As we go deep into the countryside and speak to the illiterate rustic villagers, we find some Indus monosyllabic words embedded in their speech. If we ask them some question, they reply with ta meaning 'yes'. If they have to reply in negative, they speak na with almost half or one-fourth mātrā of a. If they have to quote somebody without naming him, they say "kī do" meaning 'somebody said'. The same ta for 'yes' is also used for 'if', and with na it means 'otherwise'.

Even in Sanskrit such sentences are there, but they have been reduced in size due to accent. Thus ced 'if you say' is the reduced form of ce da of the same meaning. Of course, in Sanskrit the meaning too has contracted to 'if', but in the lively discussions in the Vedānta sūtras the original meaning is still there.

The language of the Indus inscriptions is at the isolating stage, remarkable by the presence of the monosyllabic words, forming clauses of hardly more than two or three syllables. Those monosyllabic words are alive not only in Sanskrit but even in the present day speech.

Thus jhā (attention) is uttered to make a child look at the person. The syllables ṭā and ṭho serve to indicate the exact number. The exact values of ga (injunction), gha (futurity), ha (perfect), ra (pluperfect), still continuing in the rustic dialects, have been shown elsewhere. They are the nestors of the Indic morphology, not prepared to die even after thousands of years.

As regards anybody who may appreciate my work, I say:

utpatsyate mama tu ko'pi samāna-dharmā
kālo hy ayaṃ nir-avadhir vipulā ca pṛthvī.

(Somebody of my nature will be born someday; the time is unlimited and the earth is vast.)

Last of all, but not the least, I thank Sri Nalin Sharma who is responsible for the publication of this book along with all the previous ones in this series.

–Madhusudan Mishra

Vijayā Daśamī
15-10-2002

Introduction

During the 19th century it was conceived by the linguists that even a language can be *made*, just as a potter makes a jar. This conception gave birth to a big giant called IE, and it is still living, though looked down upon by its own kinsmen.

An earlier assumption of the origin of a language through the isolating, agglutinative and inflexional stages was easily set aside by the reconstruction of the IE, proclaiming that what was spoken as such was irrelevant. This rude statement is against the tenets of the linguistic embryology.

A language is what we speak. It is the genuinely real thing. It should have an origin and growth like that of a grass. As the clucking of the monkeys gradually turned into articulate human sounds, by the cooperation of the places of utterance in the oral chamber (sthāna) and the articulatory organs (karaṇa) like the various parts of the tongue and the lower lip, a certain meaning was attached to each of them. As a first step, it referred to the birds, animals, etc. whose sound it echoed. Thus ka reflected in the sound of the peacock, and it was named by that syllable; ha echoed in the neighing of a horse, and it was named by that syllable; the humming of a bee was heard as bha, and it was called as such. In this way, 34 consonants and 5 short vowels (a i u e o), as supposed to exist at the beginning of the human speech, began to refer to birds and animals of daily encounter. The syllable ra was heard through the rattling of the burning fire, which was called by that name. In this way, many physical objects were named. Through the association of ideas, even non-physical objects and abstract ideas were named through specific syllables.

The long vowels began to serve as pronouns, which could be used without naming a person or thing.

Thus a small vocabulary came up in the language with a limited number of referends for all of them. The same vocabulary served as noun at one place and as verb elsewhere. If ka was for a peacock, it could also be used for 'to cry' (like a peacock); if ra was for fire, its rapid spreading throughout the forest would have given the meaning 'speed'. Thus there were as many verbs as nouns. Just as in the primitive form of the society the same man was a priest, a soldier, a farmer and a public servant, the same syllable served for all parts of speech in the primitive form of the language.

Our traditional Sanskrit lexicons of the monosyllabic words give us an idea of how a syllable referred to animals, birds and other small creatures, though the list is imperfect due to broken tradition: ka = peacock, turtle, sun; ca = moon; ña = ox; ḍha = dog; ta = breast ; da = mountain; ba = spider, water; bha = bee, light; ra = fire, speed; va = tiger, arrow; and ha = horse, sky.

The initial number of syllables would have theoretically amounted to (34 consonants x 14 vowels =) 476, referring to birds, animals, insects, physical objects and abstract ideas.

Thus, seeds were ready to the thrown on the earth, and a stage came in human speech when a small clause could be formed. Initially a subject ṇa (an animal, a creature) and a verb ra (speed) were assembled: ṇa ra = An animal goes. This may be called the isolating stage of the language. There is no grammar. A certain order of the monosyllabic words expresses the desired idea. There is no tense or mood, no question of any relationship of words in the small clauses.

Later, the clauses expanded by the import of other ideas like the object, which was placed between subject and verb: ṇa ma ṣa = the knowledge produces happiness. Still later, the oblique case was desired to be expressed, which was put at the first place, pushing the subject to the next position: ta na ṣa = from the womb gems come out. If the occasion demanded, even the verb was put at the first position, omitting the idea which was clear by the context: gā va = (the cattle) goes into the stable. To show plurality, the subject or object was repeated so many times.

Then the seeds began to multiply under the earth itself. Two consonants began to be ligatured to express the combination of ideas: ba (water) + ra (fire) = b-ra (lightning), ga (moving) + ra (fire) = g-ra (sun), etc. We can imagine, how many syllables would have sprung up.

But we are still at the isolating stage of the language. The extant texts of the Indus inscriptions appear to have just crossed the line of the isolating stage, because two or three consonant-pairs in unusually high numbers prompt us to suppose that they could not be due to chance. Certainly, the grammatical elements had begun to appear, because the Indus society was no more primitive as before.

They had already settled down on the two banks of the river which later came to be called Sarasvatī. Here they were at the stage of the language which could describe an object but could not say what it was. They called this river ṣa ra ṣa (4094) = from the nipple (mountain) flows (and) stops (at the sea). By the advancement of the language, this clause itself was reduced to sáras (pond, lake) which highlighted the river, on account of which it was later called Sarasvatī. By that time, the old culture was long past. It was the early Vedic age.

The Indus people on the bank of the river Sarasvatī had anyhow heard about the destruction of the glacial ages and the climatic changes on the earth. They had also heard about the 'big bang' and the 'glowing cloud millions of miles in diameter blossoming in the space', because they appear to describe these events through the little clauses.

By the time they had come to leave some message for us in writing, they had reached the great heights of material advancement and scientific knowledge about the universe. The excavations at many places have revealed the excellent governance and extraordinary townplanning of those people. They had no difficulty in writing message for us. Because every syllable of their language stood for certain bird, animal, fish and physical objects, they pictographed either the one or the other as convenient for them. Thus initially they represented every syllable of their language with these birds, animals, fish and physical objects. For example, ka was represented by turtle , ga by the two horns  of a bull, ca by an ant , pa by a leaf , na by a fish 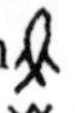 of one kind, ma by a fish  of another kind, ha by a fish  of yet another kind, ra by a man , ṇa by an armed man , ṭha by a porter , la by the hind-leg of a horse  and so on. It is pity that all animal figures could not be handed down.

When the animal figures began to look rustic with the advancement of the society, they began to invent the corresponding geometrical figures for all the syllables. Sometimes they are just improvement upon the animal figures, but sometimes they have been drawn anew. For example: ga ca pa na ma ha da bha ra ṇa ṭha la, and so on.

When their syllabary was systematised and they had become conscious linguistically, they invented an artificial but still very scientific numeral script to arrange the syllables, firstly according to qualities, then according to their places of utterance. That arrangement has come down to us, with some minor editing, by the name of the Māheśvarasūtras. The original order was as follows:

10	9	8	7	6	5	4	3	2	1
		āi	āu	ai	au	e	o	i	u
					ha	ya	va	ra	la
				ṃ	ña	ma	ṅa	ṇa	na
jha	bha	gha	ḍha	dha	ja	ba	ga	ḍa	da
cha	pha	kha	ṭha	tha	ca	ṭa	ta	ka	pa
śa	sa	ṣa						ẖa	

We can see how the number "2" alone stands for six sounds.

These three scripts have been used to write the Indus inscriptions. The signs which are easy to draw have been used more copiously than the ones which are difficult. The numeral signs also show the frequency of the syllables. The syllables which are at the first place have greater number of frequency than the ones which are at 5 or 10 on the left side.

All basic signs contain the inherent vowel a. To show the same consonant with different vowels, the animal figures have been slightly changed or modified. Thus the ant-sign, seven occurrences in all, has six variants. In case of the geometrical figures, the different vowels have been shown by the diacritical marks, although sometimes another consonant has been used to show the different vowels. For example, though the circle is for ca, it is used as a vowel-diacritic in  ṇu, and elsewhere. The numerals too show different vowels by some tricks. Thus  = ḍho, and so on. If the numerals of the same shape are used continuously, there is some intentional change in one of the two. Thus in 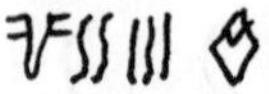 ci va ra ṣa, ra has been made wavy to avoid any confusion with ha by the two signs coming together.

Now something needs to be said on the new nomenclature, that is Sarasvatī, for the Indus valley civilisation, because this name has become debatable. The excavations had started in 1921 first of all on the banks of the river Indus and the lost civilisation which was unearthed naturally began to be called 'the Indus valley civilisation'. But now it has been ascertained that the sites on the Indus basin constitute just 5 per cent of the total area of that ancient civilisation. Now it is realised that the river Sarasvatī was the centre of that civilisation. Though it dried up by 1900 BC, it was deified as the goddess of learning, because the Aryan civilisation started on its bank. It is called Vāk (speech), Veda-garbhā (having knowledge inside), etc.

We are now fully aware of the three phases of the Indus language, which really represent the three stages in the development of the human speech. August Sleischer's 'avis akvas ka' would be 'vi ha' at the isolating stage, avi h̲a-śva cih̲a' at the agglutinative stage on the Indus basin (but h̲a extended differently elsewhere). At the inflexional stage, it would have been quite different at different places.

The north and south Indian languages are *similar* to the extent that both are at present at the agglutinative stage. They are also *dissimilar* to the extent that, while the north Indian languages have some amount of inflexion borrowed from the various phases of the inflexional ancestor, the south Indian languages have no inflexion.

If they have evolved from a common ancestor, how, standing on the same latitude typologically, are they so different?

The incident at the root of it may be stated allegorically:

Three brothers, A B and C, started on a journey. They started from X and walked upto Y through the same path. But suddenly they had to face some natural calamity, and they dispersed in haste. While A was fortunate in finding an easy path and reached the destination Z without any impediment, B and C stumbled and broke their legs.

After a pretty long time, when A was returning back from the destination in his old age, tired and exhausted, but quite differently attired, although losing much of it and also having the old rags on his body, he saw B and C limping forward in their old rags. They did not recognise one another. But A and B anyhow embraced each other to begin their new life in their respective homes. On the other hand, C retired to the forest to lead an isolated life.

On the Reading of the Indus Signs

It is amusing to recollect how the Indus signs were read one by one. As far as the memory goes, and verified from the written and dest-work records, the sign  was the first to be tentatively recognised, not through some text but by a distant reference in Pāṇini (6, 1, 64) who says that 'all initial ṣ of the Dhātupāṭha should be read s. An extraordinarily high number of occurrences of  in a small corpus of the Indus texts inspired me to read it as ṣa. It proved to be correct later. A similar attempt to locate ṇa (P.6,1,65) failed.

The following two texts, partly indentical, later suggested that the 3rd and 4th signs from the right in each line represented the same syllables:

That is to say,  and  as well as  and  represent the same syllable in each case. After a rigorous exercise it appeared that  and  represent va, and  and  represent ṇa. This was a wonderful achievement, a remarkable breakthrough.

This discovery helped the identification of the whole set of the numeral signs of specific shapes and lengths with the syllabic order of the Māheśvarasūtras. At first, the consonants could be identified as follows: 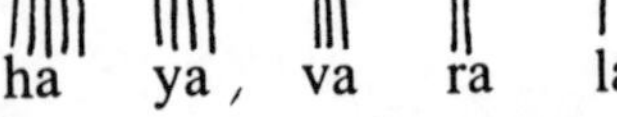

ha ya, va ra la

		ña	ma	ṅa	ṇa	na
jha	bha	gha	ḍha	dha	ja	ba	ga	ḍa	da

cha	pha	kha	ṭha	tha	ca	ṭa	ta	ka	pa

śa	sa	ṣa							ha

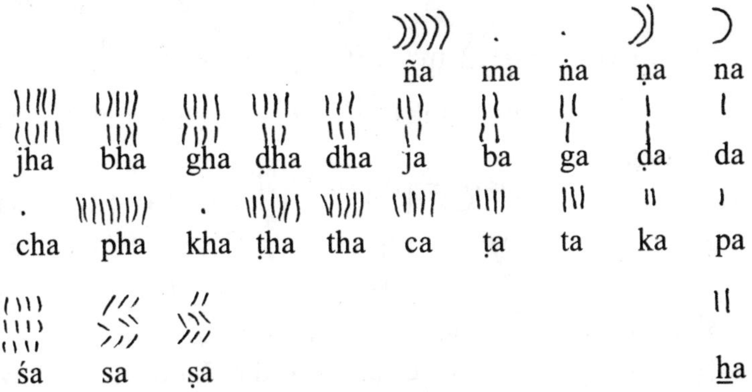

Though cha and kha are unquotable in the Indus numeral signary, it appeared that there was some editing carried out in the ur-Māheśvarasūtras: the places of cha and kha as well as sa and ṣa were interchanged by the Sanskrit school.

Even the vowels, though not properly represented by the numerals, could be recognised through their number going upto 7. Because Pāṇini has highlighted u   among the vowels (P.1,2,27), it was supposed that the vowel series began with   u in the Indus syllabary. The following vowel series was thus provisionally identified:

āi	āu	ai	au	e	o	i	u

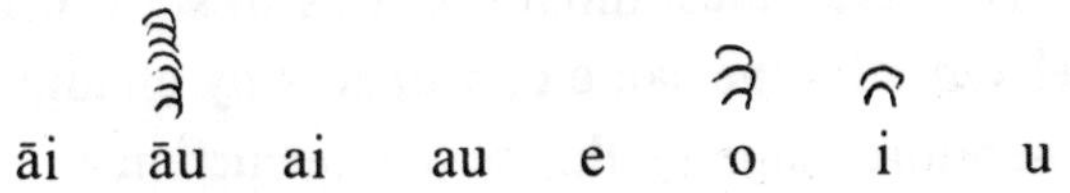

The inherent a of the consonants has not been indicated through the numeral signs. But the pattern of the numeral vowels helped to identify the diacritical marks increasing in number for the respective vowels:

ṣu	ṣi	ṣo	ṣe

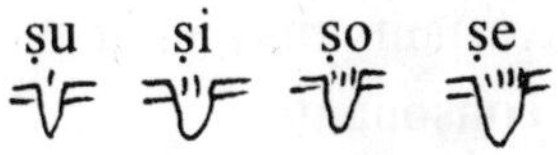

The numeral signs were of great help in the identification of other signs in duplicate texts:

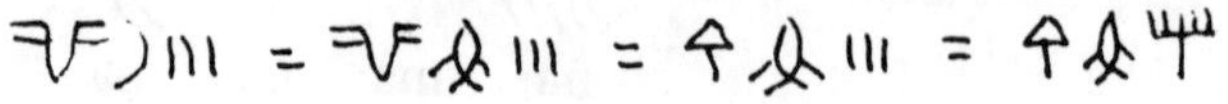

It proved that 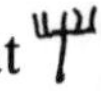 = ta,  = ṣa, and  =na.

Similarly,

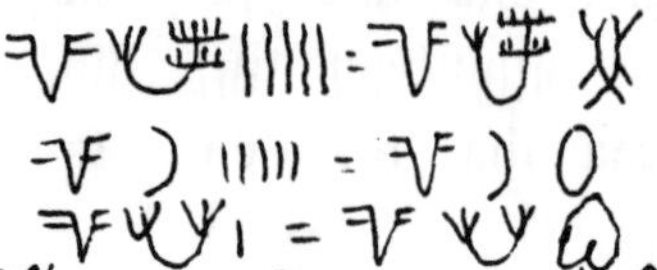

ha lī ṣa

ca na ṣa

pa ka ṣa

showed that  =ha,  =ca, and  =pa.

By this time it was clear that the Indus texts have appeared in three scripts: animal figures, geometrical figures and numerals. Because the primitive vocabulary of the language was monosyllabic and each syllable stood for animals, birds, little insects and some physical objects, the simplest of them were portrayed for each syllable. The 34 consonants with 14 vowels could have amounted to 476 syllables and there should have been so many syllables for them in the beginning, but gradually they were restricted to 34 symbols for consonants with the vowel a, and five for the simple vowels, other syllables made by diacritics and through ligatures.

However, the animal figures still show different syllables related with the same consonants by changing their shapes. Therefore, among the seven occurrences of the ant-sign, there are six variants. They certainly show the consonant c with different vowels. Similarly, the leaf-sign, ascetic-sign, dog-sign and drum-sign have variants and they certainly stand for different vowels attached with those consonants. Even the geometrical signs having the remarkable different variants may indicate different vowels attached with those consonants.

While transisting from the animal figures into the geometrical figures, some signs have changed completely, while in some other cases the change is just pulsating, showing that they are the same sounds:

Animal figures: 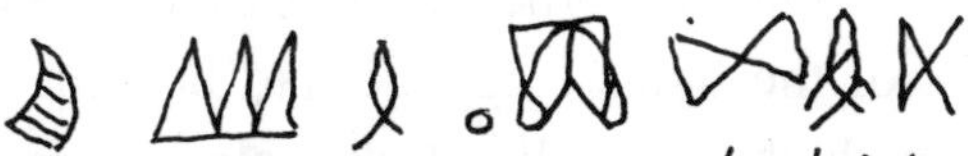

Geometrical figures: 

In the geometrical figures the variation has been caused by the different hands of the scribes. The rhomboid changing into oval, and vice versa, stands for the same sound: 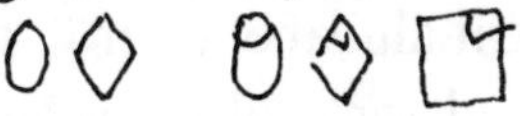

When the animal figures gradually changed into the geometrical figures, there were two different sets of the same Indus syllabary: each phoneme had two symbols.

When the qualities of sounds and their places of utterance were accurately determined, the artificial numeral figures were invented in the most scientific way. We can see through the list of the numerals that only "2" stands for six sounds through its different shapes, apart from one as diacritic for i.

Although the animal and geometrical figures of the Indus signs were gradually being recognised through the help of the numerals, besides through their own mutual help, there was a very startling revelation that the decayed, wornout and reduced vocables of the early Vedic language reflected in the clauses and phrases of the Indus texts.

The first to be so identified was the sign  along with  in the text  which was abruptly read rau ra. It appeared to reflect in the rare Vedic vocable rūrá (the heat of the fever). On the basis of the meaning of this word, the Indus clause was interpreted thus: the fire burns. This chance bullet hit the bull's eye.

On the border of Indus and Vedic, the inflexional stage of the Indus language had become accented on account of which the earlier Indus clauses and phrases were sharply reduced in size. Phonetically, ṭha was dentalised and deaspirated to ta, ra was reduced to ṛ, and the final or medial vowel was generally lost. That is why, the Vedic vocables look like emaciated ascetics before the Indus clauses and phrases.

Many syllables of the Sanskrit alphabet refer to animals, birds, etc. as their meanings, and some of them have been pictographed in the Indus signary:

da mountain  , bha bee  , ḍha dog  , ba spider  , sa bird  , pa leaf  , ka turtle  , ḍa drum  , ta breast  , va arrow  , ṣa nipple  , ca moon  .

These pictographs were provisionally identified with those syllables, and the clauses which they made, also found in the Indus texts, wonderfully reflected in the wornout and decayed Vedic vocables:

 na bha ṣa nábhas 'cloud, sky'

 ta na ṣa tánas 'offspring'

 va na ra vanar in vanar-gu, -ṣad.

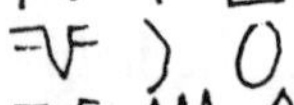 ca na sa cánas 'delight'

 ha da sa sádas 'place'

When so much progress was made in reading the Indus signs, the Indus texts themselves set out in search of the wornout Vedic vocables:

Then 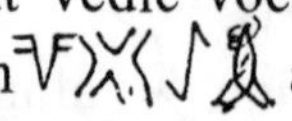 appeared to be read śa ma yo ṣa, which reflected in the Vedic śám yós (wellbeing and welfare); 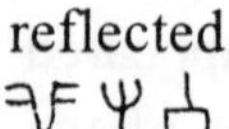 va na sa reflected in vánas (in vánas-páti), and so on.

Even the geometrical figures helped to identify the animal figures, and vice versa: na bha sa is identical with where = ; = , where =

In identical texts, the duplicates were also detected:

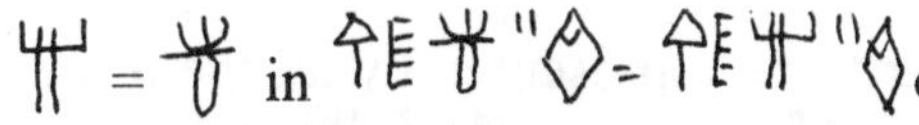
ci<u>h</u>a śa gha ṣa

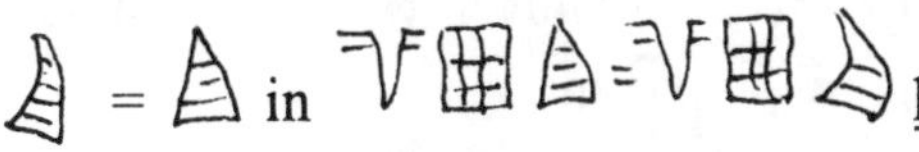
<u>h</u>a nu ṣa

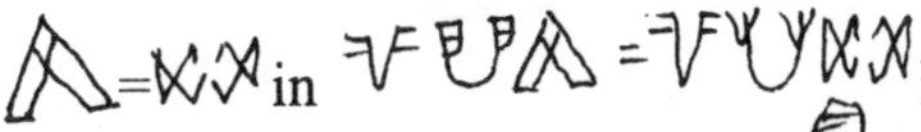
ī ka ṣa

The hind-leg of a horse was identified with la through a Hindi word lathār (strike by the hind-leg), and some wonderful texts were read: la ṭha (time disc) means: the time rolls on, which appears as ṛtá (the regular order of time) with various meanings in Sanskrit.

The following texts show the different values of the individual signs, indicating that there were no strict graphic rules in this regard:

= ro/rāu in ro ka ṣa Vedic rokas 'fire'
= yū in yū ṣi (in Paśupati text) Vedic yūs 'soup'
= re in ci re (in Dholavira text) Vedic cire = ciram
= bū in bū jña ṣu Mod. Persian bū 'smell'
= tū in ba u tū Hindi botū 'he-goat'
= bu in bu la bu la <u>h</u>a Hindi bulabulā 'bubble'
= ī in ī śa (He punishes) īśa (the lord Siva)
= bī in ra bī ṣu Vedic ṛbīsa 'an abyss'
= cī in ra cī ṣa Sanskrit ṛcīṣa'a frying pan'
= jī in ra jī ṣu Vedic ṛjīṣa

Some texts show that a whole clause has been abridged as a word; rā rā rā ma Vedic rāma 'a black man'. On this basis some signs capped from two sides may be taken to be the long vowel ā:  kā from ka,  = ṇā from  ṇa.

In some cases a consonant becomes a mark for vowel:  = nu,  = tu, 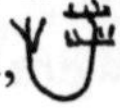 = lī

Some syllables appear to be represented by all the three scripts; e.g. ha 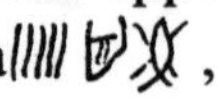, h̲a 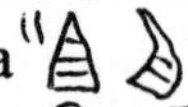. Thus 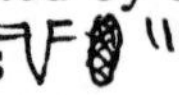 = ha nu ṣa , that is,  = 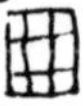 nu.

Signs Distinguished from the Graphic Variants

Mahadevan has morphologically classified the signs of the Indus script in nine groups, but broadly the signs can be distinguished simply as (1) the animal figures, (2) the geometrical figures and (3) the numerals. Some figures representing the physical objects too may be taken under the animal figures; e.g. 230 the mountain. The signs which increase in strokes should be considered as numerals; e.g. the signs from 287 to 298 and those from 312 to 315, apart from the ones which have already been grouped as numerals (86-121). Though some animal figures have turned geometrical in course of their evolution, they are still recognisable as animal figures; e.g., 1,12,17. The mountain has been drawn geometrically, but it has been further improved in 367. Some geometrical figures differ only slightly from the animal figures from which they have evolved; e.g. 204 from 205. Some animal figures have been drawn geometrically from the very beginning; e.g. 225 which has been slightly modified as 211 for some cognate sound. A rhomboid turning into oval and vice versa is rather a duplicate than a variant, which has rightly been listed separately; e.g. 261 is not different from 373, 380 is not different from 245. On account of appearing in identical surroundings, 347 does not appear to be different from 358, or 174 from 175.

But some signs have been supposed to have variants. Out

of 419 signs in Mahadevan's sign-list, 179 signs have variants totalling 641 forms. That is to say, 641 variants have been normalised among 179 signs. This normalisation has sharply reduced the number of signs, which otherwise would have touched thousand.

A count of the number of signs in other writings reveals that the alphabetic systems have much less than 50 symbols, the syllabic systems have much less than 100 symbols, but the logographic systems have much beyond 500 symbols. Based on this criterion, many scholars try to read the Indus inscriptions logographically, because apparently the number of signs in the Indus inscriptions goes beyond 500.

But proceeding with this view-point we may go astray, because there may be other grounds for a language having many signs. It has been stated earlier that there are three broad divisions of the signs in the Indus script. The writing would have started with the animal figures. Gradually, it would have transited to the geometrical figures. Thus the number of signs would have been doubled.

If the numerals are assembled together in groups, the same "number" may appear in various shapes:

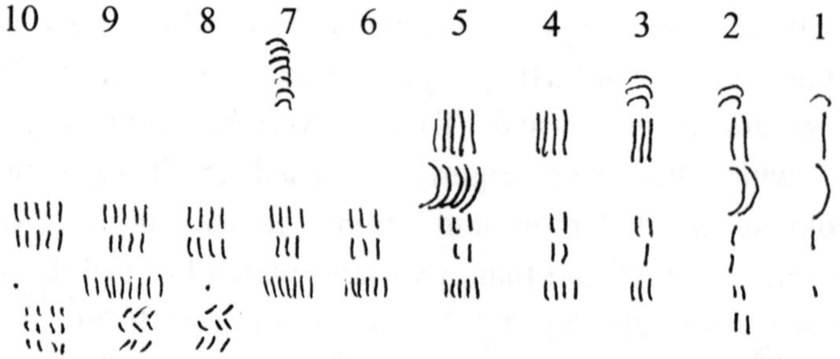

It was after some reflection that the syllabic order of the Māheśvarasūtras was put upon the series of numerals and, very surprisingly, each numeral sign was identified with the specific syllable of the Māheśvarasūtras:

10	9	8	7	6	5	4	3	2	1
			āu	.	.	.	o	i	u
					ha	ya	va	ra	la
					na	.	.	na	na
jha	bha	gha	dha	dha	ja	ba	ga	da	da
.	pha	.	tha	tha	ca	ta	ta	ka	pa
śa	sa	ṣa						ẖa	

There were some anomalies in the order of the vowels and sibilants, which were resolved later.

Then it appeared that the Indus inscriptions have been handed down simultaneously in three scripts, namely animal figures, geometrical figures and numerals. It is remarkable that the various shapes of the numeral "2" have given not less than six syllables.

As one-third of the basic syllables was identified through the syllabic order of the Māheśvarasūtras, the animal and geometrical figures have been identified in the duplicate and triplicate texts through the help of the numerals; e.g.  ta na ṣa could hardly be different from 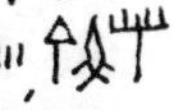

On this theoretical basis, the Indus inscriptions represent the syllabic system, and the attempt to read the signs logographically may become fruitless. Mahadevan's seeing the agglutinative Dravidian in this grammar-less isolating Indus has no logic, and others seeing the inflexional Sanskrit in it "andhaṃ tamaḥ praviśanti".

It has been suggested that the signs have variants due to the different hands of the scribes. To a certain extent, this is justifiable, but the ant-sign (57) has seven occurrences in all, and there are six variants. This cannot be due to the different hands of the scribes. On examination it appears that, because the animal signs do not admit diacritical marks, the different shapes of the same animal indicate the same consonant with different vowels. Here it appears that the normalisation of signs is not a good idea and each variation should be faithfully recorded.

Because some signs used in small numbers have proportionately a great number of variants, they are to be reckoned as consonants with different vowels, notably:

48	 has, out of	168 occurrences,	9 variants
49		2	, 2
50		8	, 4
51		105	, 7
53		130	, 3
54		19	, 4
56		8	, 3
84		8	, 5

Even the geometrical signs have numerous variants, and it has been possible to examine the presence of the same consonant with different vowels too. However, we have to be careful in case of the geometrical figures, because here the different hands of the scribes may bring differences.

Though diacritics have been used to mark the different vowels even in case of the animal figures and numerals, it is prominently so in case of the geometrical figures. If there is no possibility of adding diacritical marks in the geometrical figures the internal strokes therein have been increased or decreased to show the different vowels attached with the consonants.

Just as the plural had been made by repeating the signs so many times at the initial stage of the language, the long vowels have been shown by attaching the vowel-signs from two sides. Thus the signs joined from two sides are clearly vowels; e.g. 16, 24, 29 and 217-8.

In the geometrical signs, the variation has been carried out more by the changing number of strokes than by changing the shape

169	 has	12 variants
171		4
173		4
175		4
176		10
178		6

It is probable that  is not the variant of , though  may be the variant of the latter.

The Ur-Māheśvarasūtras

While systematising the Indus phonology, the ancient phoneticians had two ideas in their mind. On the one hand, they considered the qualities of the groups of phonemes to be the most important, for which they invented different sizes or shapes of the numerals:

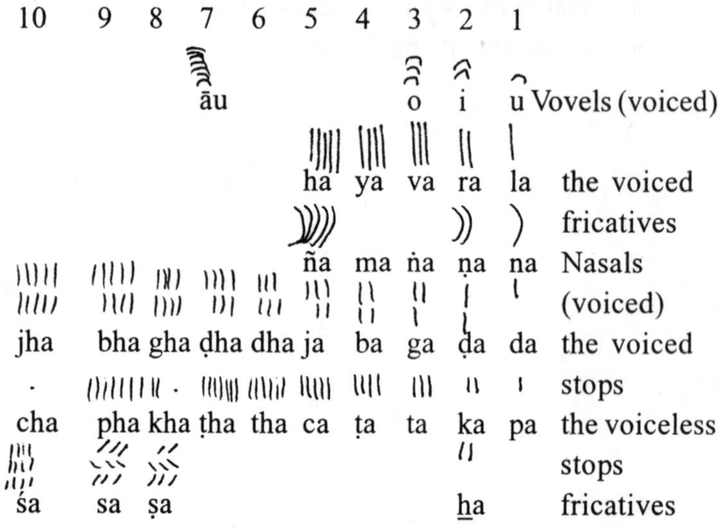

10 9 8 7 6 5 4 3 2 1
āu o i u Vovels (voiced)
ha ya va ra la the voiced
fricatives
ña ma ṅa ṇa na Nasals
(voiced)
jha bha gha ḍha dha ja ba ga ḍa da the voiced
stops
cha pha kha ṭha tha ca ṭa ta ka pa the voiceless
stops
śa sa ṣa ha fricatives

On the other hand, while they wanted to maintain the order of the places of utterance of the phonemes, they had also the relative frequencies of the phonemes in their mind. Due to this double thinking, the order of the places of utterance had often to be guillotined.

The nasals and the voiced stops presented the normal order according to the places of utterance (from right to left: dental cerebral-velar-labial-palatal), but it was not observed in case of the semivowels and sibilants, as judged from the increasing number of strokes from right to left.

In case of the voiceless stops, there is more irregularity. The Indus-phoneticians themselves put pa ka in a separate group with smaller strokes, highlighting their relative frequency. Thus ta-ṭa-ca tha-ṭha-cha (dental-cerebral-palatal) do not follow the previous order. Then the Sanskrit school took the licence for some further change, taking into account the Sanskrit phonetic system, and the places of cha and kha were interchanged. Thus Pāṇini reads them, from left to right, in the following way: kha pha cha ṭha tha ca ṭa ta, ka pa. In Mahadevan's list of signs, the numerals with small strokes, 10 cha and 8 kha not represented at all and 9 pha only once, show how the voiceless aspirates were negligible in Indus phonology. The phonemes cha-ṭha-tha and ca-ṭa-ta make a significant group, having the corresponding sibilants ś-ṣ-s, and have been flanked on both sides by kha pha and ka pa, having no corresponding sibilants.

The original order of the Indus vowels has undergone drastic revision. The Indus vowel series began with u, and then i o e au ai au ai followed it, though only u i o and āu are quotable. But diacritically at least four vowels are definitely quotable: 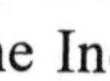 ṣu 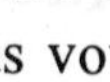 ṣi  ṣo 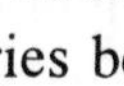 ṣe. The vowels (u i o e au ai āu āi) were broken into 4 groups (1. u i 2. o e 3. au ai 4. āu āi), and then each time it was read in the reverse order, the first group beginning with a inherently present in all consonants, the second group which had disappeared being replaced by ṛ l (which had newly appeared), the third group contracted as e o, and the fourth group too contracted as ai au.The edited Indus phonology, known as the Māheśvarasūtras, is the following:

1.* a i u 2. ṛ l 3. e o 4. ai au 5. ha ya va ra 6. la 7. ña ma ṅa ṇa na 8. jha bha 9. gha ḍha dha 10. ja ba ga ḍa da 11. kha pha cha ṭha tha ca ṭa ta 12. ka pa 13. śa ṣa sa 14. ẖa

The greatest divergence of the Paninean Māheśvarasūtras from the ur-Māheśvarasūtras is the inclusion of the vowels ṛ and ḷ and the omission of the outgoing e and o, the contraction of ai āi au āu to e ai o au, the interchange of the places of ch and kh as well as ṣ and s being just minor events.

Upto the last days of the agglutinative Indus there was no trace of ṛ, much less of ḷ. But on the threshold of the inflexional stage, the accent on the neighbouring syllable weakened ra to ṛ. The syllable la had first of all to undergo rhotacism, then it was weakened to ṛ. But the emergence of this ṛ was just like the flash of lightning. As soon as it was born it was dead. However, it showed its presence in some words for a long time, due to which some other cases of ṛ arose analogically. In the languages other than Vedic, it is non-existent, a liquid r supported by some vowel from one side.

Though the voiced form of śa ṣa sa also arose secondarily, they were no sooner born than dead, their presence remaining only in the mind of the speaker. After ā, a z was lost without any trace, but in other cases ẓ and ź left their impression.

We just wonder why the voiceless stops, represented by small strokes, were put in two groups of "ch ph kh ṭh th c ṭ t" (represented by the ordinary small strokes) and k p (represented by the smaller strokes). It is conspicuously

---

*Pānini had to apologise for not beginning the vowel series with u in the form of highlighting u instead of a to show the length of the vowels: ūzkālo'j jhrasva-dīrgha-plutaḥ p. 1, 2, 27.

clear that the phonemes at the first position show greater frequency and those at the end show least frequency. But in case of the voiceless stops, p and k had as much frequency as t ṭ. Therefore, the size of the strokes for p k was made smaller. Pāṇini just obeyed the order of the older phoneticians, but he also interchanged the places of ch and kh to keep kh ph and k p at the two ends of the other voiceless stops - ch ṭh th c ṭ t - having the corresponding sibilants ś ṣ s. This also necessitated the change in the original order of the sibilants: ś s ṣ.

The Indus Syllabary

The presence of 419 signs (or more, taking the graphic variant into account) gives the impression that the signs are logographic. It turns out to be a hoax if we realise that there are three versions of the same script, namely the animal figures, geometrical figures and the numerals. Moreover, because most of the animal figures did not admit the diacritics for other vowels, often widely divergent signs were invented for different syllables from the same consonant. E.g., the ant-sign has seven occurrences in all, but it has six variants, each one of them for specific c-syllables. It is also possible that, initially, there were as many pictographs as different syllables from the same consonant (e.g. ka kā ki kī ku ku, etc.), representing animal, bird, insect, physical object, etc. expressed by those syllables (theoretically not more than 34 consonants x 14 vowels = 476). E.g., the fish sign  for ha shows additional strokes in 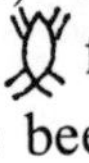 for another h-syllable. Though the five bird-signs have been listed, two of them having several variants, they probably represent the same (s-) consonant with specific vowels, apart from the fact that the bracketed bird-sign also is one of such syllables, probably showing the length of the vowel in question. As a rule, 14 variants of an animal sign are admissible for different syllables connected with one consonant (e.g. ka kā ki kī ku kū ke kē ko kō kai kau kāi kāu). The signs with diacritical marks, e.g. 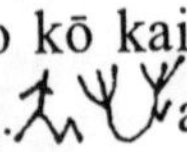 are another factor for increase in the number of signs.

As a matter of fact, the basic signs cannot be more than (34 consonants + 14 vowels x 3 =) 144, including also the numerals.

The multiplicity of the animal signs was to some extent carried to the geometrical signs, though in case of numerals it was restrained.

The animal and geometrical figures are shown below separately in the order of the numerals shown in the previous chapter.

The animal figures:

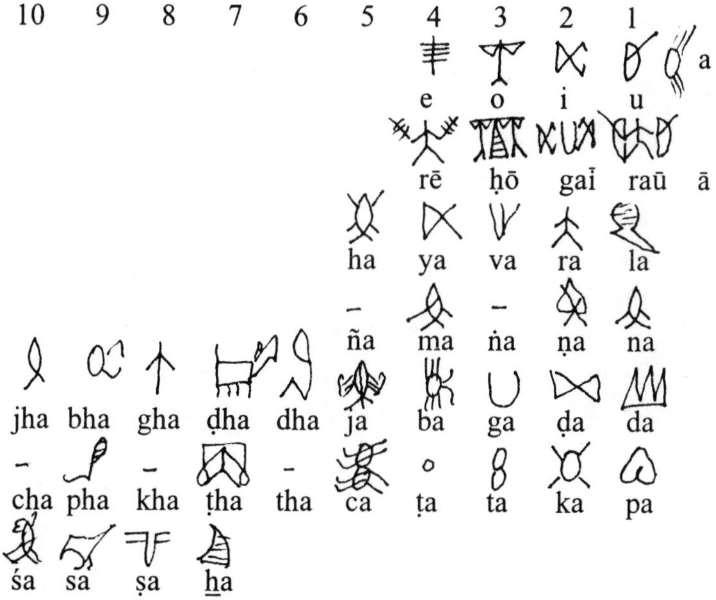

The geometrical figures:

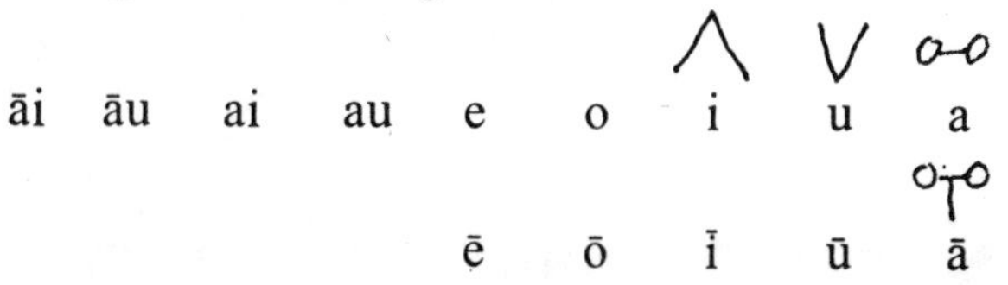

ha ya va ra la
ña ma ṅa ṇa na
jha bha gha ḍha dha ja ba ga ḍa da
cha pha kha ṭha tha ca ṭa ta ka pa
śa sa ṣa h̲a

Some Phonetic Rules

The redrafting of the original Indus phonology to the stage of the Māheśvarasūtras had been occasioned by the phonetic change taking place in the language as it passed from Indus to Sanskrit.

1. The Indus ra and la had been weakend to ṛ/ḷ on account of the accent on the neighbouring syllable:

ratu (Av): ṛtû

la ṭha: ṛtá

2. The Indus e o were gradually lost by the time of the RV. They were replaced by the newly developed ṛ ḷ in the Māheśvarasūtra. Similarly, ai au and āi āu had contracted to e o and ai au respectively, as shown in the Māheśvarasūtra.

3. There was a general tendency of dentalisation of the cerebrals. It was known to the phoneticians of the RV-Prātiśākhya who say that 'the dentals are really the alveolars'.

Thus the cerebral ṣ has everywhere changed to s:

ṣa ra ṣa: sáras

ta na ṣa: tánas

4. Though the initial ṣ and ṇ of the original verbs had changed to s and n by the beginning of the Vedic language, the traditional Dhātupāṭha was continuing with ṣ and ṇ at the initial position. Therefore, Pāṇini had to prescribe that all the initial ṣ and ṇ of the (Indus) Dhātupāṭha (carried to Sanskrit) should be replaced by s and n.

5. Due to accent on the neighbouring syllable, the following or the preceding syllable had to lose the vowel:

ṇa ga: nág

pa ka ṣa: pakṣá

6. The non-initial ṭh had been dentalised and also deaspirated:

ṣa ṭha: sát

ṣa-ṭha: (ṣ-ṭha) > s-tá (Hindi thā).

7. Though there were voiceless and voiced h in Indus, by the time of the Vedic language the voiceless pronunciation of h was considered to be a fault. Therefore, the initial h of Indus was either lost (if followed by a sibilant or r) or changed to s*:

haṣṭa: aṣṭa

haśva: aśva

harva: arvā

but

hapta: sapta

ha ṭha ṣa: satás

8. Though the accent had a tendency to voice the following stop and to cause the following s to go, there are also exceptions to it:

va ṇa ṭha: vanád

but

vánat > vart (vṛt)

ma ṇā ṣa: manā

but

ta na ṣa: tánas.

The loss of the final s may be due to the preceding long vowel.

---

* Though the Santhal language too is said to have both the voiced and voiceless h (Bodding, The Santhal dictionary, p. I, III), in Mundari it is retained whereas in Santhal it is lost initially (ato:hatu). This silent h is probably the voiceless one, having the same fate in Vedic.

The Verbs of the Isolating Indus

The Vedic language is genetically related with Indus, and both are at the two ends of the linguistic development, typologically the Vedic being inflexional and the language of the extant Indus texts being isolating. The intermediate agglutinative stage is remarkably missing. Because the stream of the linguistic development is the same, the invisible underground agglutinative current appears in the inflexional territory of Sanskrit. That is to say, the agglutinative stage of Indus is conspicuously visible in the inflexional Sanskrit, though it has been very often ingeniously explained as being the feature of the inflexional language.

The expression adhi-hari (= harau, in Hari) is a typically agglutinative formation, but it has been explained as an adverbial compound by Pāṇini (2,1,6). The other cases expressed agglutinatively, e.g. accusative by the particle iti (devam = deva iti), instrumental and ablative by dvārā (bila-dvārā = bilena, bilāt), dative by kṛte (asmat-kṛte = asmabhyam), have been treated by Pāṇini as general compounds or syntactical devices. His formulation in this respect is that any inflected word can be compounded with another inflected form (P 2,1 4). As a matter of fact, a good part of Sanskrit morphology belongs to the mother state, namely agglutinative. Often the agglutinative Sanskrit is as natural as the inflexional Sanskrit (a-gaccha-t: gacchati sma). It appears that the inflexional Sanskrit language has been simplified by the agglutinative technique. The inflexional Sanskrit has the liking to employ its inflected elements agglutinatively. Thus gacchati itself is turned into past and future by adding sma and purā respectively.

In some cases, the agglutinative feature of Sanskrit has been overshadowed by the host of inflexional elements. The so-called past augment a-, ā- before vowels and some consonants, is a special feature of the past verbal forms in Sanskrit and, at the agglutinative stage, before the persons and numbers came to be distinguished, it was the only element to show the past tense, e.g., in ā-ha (past-say) = said, ā-ṣa (past-be) = (there) was. Later the past endings reduced the importance of the augment, so that it was often dropped.

The verbs of the isolating Indus, distinguishing past tense by means of the prefix ā at the agglutinative stage, came down to the inflexional stage in their original form; e.g.

ā-ha
ā-sa for ā-ṣa
ā-na for ā-ṇa
ā-śa
ā-va
ā-ra

But they were understood differently at the inflexional stage, being the result of reduplication of the newly conceived verbs ah, as, an, av and ar (ṛ) respectively, explained as Perfect 3p. sg-forms by the Sanskrit grammarians. That is to say, the simple ā-ha was split as a-ah-a, and ah was conceived as a verb at the inflexional stage.

Through this simple process we can conceive at least the following verbs at the isolating stage: ha (to say), ṣa (to be). ṇa (to breathe), śa (to eat), va (to protect) and ra (to go).

Following this pattern, we can guess that all Sanskrit verbs beginning with a were represented by the following consonant with the vowel a. That is to say, at the isolating stage of Indus, ac (to bend) was ca, aj (to drive) was ja, aṭ (to walk) was ṭa[1], at (to go) was ta, ad (to eat) was da, and so on. As a matter of fact, the 34 consonants of the ur-Māheśvarasūtras were the basic verbs at the isolating stage of Indus. Then each consonant with a, bending towards i, u, e, o would have multiplied the number of verbs[2].

Some of the agglutinative verbal forms have turned up as suffixes in Sanskrit. Thus ca (to be, take place) made a pluperfect form ca-ra (had been, had taken place). It was used in the clauses ku cara, go cara at the agglutinative stage. When these clauses contracted as kucara[3] and gocara[4] at the inflexional stage, they became, more or less, obscure semantically. The pluperfect form cara was, however, noted as a secondary suffix by Pāṇini in the sense of "bhūtapūrva" (P 5,3,53).

The verb ma 'to grow old' made a Perfect form ma-ha (has grown old), which was used in the clause tata maha (the father has grown old). Later the clause contracted as tatāmaha (grandfather) and its-maha part was conceived as suffix in pitāmaha, etc. Needless to say, many such small verbal forms of the agglutinative Indus could not endure and they disappeared from the language.

By such penetrating enquiries into the Vedic morphology, we can bring to light the verbs of the isolating stage of Indus with their intended meanings.

Notes and Reference

1. As in the primitive constitution of the society the same man could do all works, in the primitive form

of the language the same word could serva as all parts of speech. Every syllable could be a verb at one place and a noun at another place. It is interesting to note that ṭa, from which the verb aṭ (to walk) could emerge in Sanskrit, is still available in some rustic dialect in the sense of 'leg'. If we explore the rustic dialects of India, all syllables may be found to have specific meanings which belong to the isolating stage of Indus.

2. With the five basic vowels (a i u e o), short and long, we can imagine nearly 340 verbs at the isolating stage of the Indus language. Later they would have been extended by different syllables, some of which were treated as affix at the inflexional stage e.g. ra-cha-ti: ṛcháti. The same syllable was also extended by some consonant at the beginning; e.g. p-ra-cha-ti: pṛ-chá-ti.
3. The form kucara was so tightly attached, also semantically obscure, that the editors of the pada-text could not analyse it.
4. The word gocara is still semantically obscure in itself, though widely used in Sanskrit.

Indus, the Earliest Human Speech

From the preceding accounts of the Indus language it appears that it was a sentence-language. That is to say, there were only sentences in the Indus language.

An object was indicated through a clause, that is, through a verb. There was no word for 'a river', but there was only the clause 'it flows'. In Sanskrit, a sentence is defined as 'having a finite verb' (eka-tiṅ vākyam), which also means the verb itself. Apparently, the Indus being a sentence-language looks difficult to be conceived, but we know that the world had begun with 'action' and, therefore, the human speech too was initially only a verb. The most primitive form of the human speech would have been like this.

Though, typologically, the isolating is said to be the most primitive and the first stage in the development of the human speech, this stage also started with a verb. That is to say, a traveller was called 'he travels'. It was only some time later that a subject was made to precede it. At a still later stage, an oblique case was made to precede the subject, or an object was made to follow the same. Thus this primitive language would have evolved through the following stages: 1. verb 2. subject + verb 3. oblique case + subject + verb or subject + object + verb. The search for such a primitive language has never been made, and if such a language appears to stand before us, we are likely to disbelieve or ignore it.

As far as the Indus inscriptions have been read and understood by me, it is that type of the primitive language. Its every syllable is a word: only a verb, if it is alone; a subject + a verb, if in pair; and so on.

That is to say, a river is indicated by na 'it flows', though later na itself came to designate ' a river', as also all other verbs. The same inscriptions further proceed to say that just a verb was not enough, and it was usually preceded by a subject, or it was also reinforced by some other idea. Thus an animal was specified as ṇa ra 'a living object goes'; a river was further specified as na da 'it flows (and) makes indistinct noise'. The river which later came to be callled Sarasvatī was expressed as ṣa ra ṣa 'from the mountain flows (and) stops (at the sea). We can go on imagining thousands of such small clauses on the same model.

If the Māheśvara-sūtras at the beginning of the Pāṇini's grammar is supposed to represent the phonology of the Indus language, we can measure its competence regarding the vocabulary. The 33 or 34 consonants (h y v r l, ñ m ṅ ṇ n, jh bh gh ḍh dh j b g ḍ d, kh ph ch ṭh th c ṭ t k p, ś ṣ s ẖ) with 14 vowels (a ā i ī u ū e ē o ō ai āi au āu) would have initially created 476 syllables. Later, the 33 consonants, conjoined with one another and bearing 14 vowels, would have created 15246 conjunct syllables, so that the total number of syllables would have been raised to 15708. This is, however, the competence of the language. Its performance is restricted to 419 or much less, because graphically there are many duplicates and triplicates of the same syllable.

For how much duration of time this sentence-language continued, we cannot say. Gradually, the verbs changed into substantives, and bisyllabic and trysyllabic clauses began to emerge. Even several such clauses combined in the same text. Later, even affix elements began to appear, announcing the beginning of the agglutinative stage in the language.

At least the affix-ga for injunctive and -gha for future are quite conspicuously present in the texts, -ṭha for past is also present in some doubtful circumstances, and the following affixes are in our imaginatin: -ha for perfect, -ra for pluperfect the prefix ā- for past, and so on. They have been detailed elsewhere.

The sentence-language disappeared at the early stage of its origin. But the materials of that phase continued to be present. While the verbs changed into substantives in their original form and they were meticulously preserved in the traditional lexicons, the bisyllabic and trisyllabic clauses began to contract, changing the clauses into phrases. For example, ṇa (animal) ra (goes) began to contract as ṇara 'a walking animal', gā (goes) va (into the pen) as gāva 'going into the pen', and so on. These phrases were later semantically contracted as specific lexemes: ṇara 'an animal, man', gāva 'a bull, cattle', etc. These lexemes too have been meticulously preserved in the traditional lexicons, but their meanings are not always attested in the literature. They have been, however, compiled in the modern Sanskrit dictionaries with the mark L (lexicon). The word gāvī has been quoted by Patañjali as the dialectal form of go-. Pāṇini quotes Sphoṭāyana who knew another form gava-. All these dialectal forms end with vowels.

The developing language did not stop at the aggultinative stage, which was still monotonous. It reached the inflexional stage, characterised by the appearance of the accent. The monotonous agglutivative turned into the accented inflexional, on account of which the size of the words was sharply reduced.

That is to say, the agglutinative plural form ṇara-ṣa became ṇáras, gāva-ṣa became gāvas, etc. At this stage, the words were analysed differently: ṇaras as nár-as, gā́vas as gāv-as, etc. Thus, new bases like nar/nṛ, gāu/gau/go, etc. sprang up. They have been detailed elsewhere.

Though náras (RV 7,103,7c) formally belongs to the inflexional Vedic, semantically it is still limping at the agglutinative Indus stage, where it means just 'animal, creature'.

Even some verbal forms have turned up as secondary suffixes in the later phase of the language. Thus the agglutinative clause tata maha (the father has grown old) later contracted as tatāmaha (grandfather), its -maha part becoming the secondary suffix in pitā-maha, etc. The verbal form ca-ra (had been, had taken place) was recognised by Pāṇini as a secondary suffix in the sense of 'former'. Many secondary suffixes of Sanskrit are of this origin.

Though the inflexional languages are held to represent the highest stage of evolution and the most perfect form of human communication, it is at the analytic stage that the material culture has advanced to such an extent. Though any remark may be hasty and presumptuous, the inflexional stage appears to be related with the philosophical or spiritual height of the culture, the analytic state is related with the material culture. Also, though the terms 'isolating' and 'analytic' are confounded in relation to language, some distinction has to be made. The isolating is the very early stage in the origin and development of the language, but the analytic is the very advanced stage in the development of the same. At the isolating stage there is no grammar, but at the analytic stage, the grammar of the language is in a very devastated state.

The isolating and analytic stages do not stand on the same latitude of the linguistic development, because the isolating is the great-grandfather of the analytic which, though having little grammar, has also some amount of inflexion borrowed from the inflexional ancestor. All these linguistic terms may be put in the following scale of ascent and descent:

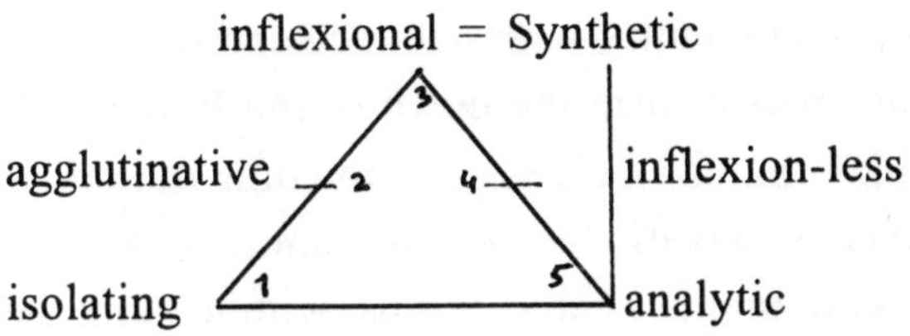

Many of the modern languages of the world, after descending from the inflexional stage, stood at the analytic stage, but before they could come on record, they had moved to the next round of the agglutinative stage, also having some amount of inflexion. In short, they are, at the same time, analytic, agglutinative and inflexional. This is not the case with the Dravidian and Santhal languages. They are typically agglutinative, having no inflexion worthy of name, because they have never come through the inflexional stage.

Though both isolating and analytic are followed by agglutinative in their development, the two agglutinative stages are as much different as the isolating and analytic. The isolating has no ancestor. It is the seed. The analytic is the fossilised tree, where new leaves have begun to appear.

A Linguistic History of India

India is one country with one race and one language. At least it was really so in the dawn of the Indian history. As the articulate human voice began to come out on the banks of the river Sarasvatī, the people communicated with one another with monosyllabic words without any grammar. They made little clauses with a subject and a verb; e.g. ṇa (a creature) ra (speed) meaning 'a creature walks'. Just as the same man in that primitive society was a priest, a soldier, a farmer and a public servant, the same syllable could be used as any part of speech. This was the socalled isolating stage of their language. If they wanted to show plurality of the subject and object and the intensification or repetition of the verbal idea, they just repeated it so many times. There was no tense or mood, the context showing it.

Then the cases began to be specified through the position of the words, when the clause expanded in length. The subject + verb being the initial form of the clause, an object began to be interposed in the middle: ṇa ma ṣa = The knowledge produces happiness. Later, in extended clauses, the oblique case assumed the first position, pushing the subject and verb further. Still later, a clause could consist of any order of words. For example, in gā va (goes into the stable) there is only the verb followed by the oblique case. In bī ja (in the water it grows) the order has been reversed.

It was still the isolating stage of the language, present in the extent Indus inscriptions.

Later, the society advanced in culture. It spread geographically upto the river Indus in the west, Gangā in the east, Tāpti in the south, and Sutlej, Beas, etc. in the north. The modern excavations have exposed their wonderful advancement in science and technology. Then they also needed a language in the written form.

As all the syllables referred to birds, animals, insects and physical objects in the surrounding in their own contexts, the simplest figures of them began to represent the respective sounds. Thus all the 33 consonants with at least 5 vowels (a i u e o) were pictographed to give the language a written form. Later the same animal figures could be shaped differently to show the different vowels.

Gradually the animal figures began to turn into geometrical figures in the hands of the different scribes. Therefore, they soon devised the corresponding geometrical figures for all the animal figures. Here they were also able to devise diacritical marks for different vowels instead of showing the different shapes of the same animals for the different vowels.

When the language was still at the isolating stage, the sounds were exactly determined as to their qualities and places of utterance. They devised the artificial numeral script in the most scientific way, which was transmitted to the later grammatical tradition by the name of the Māheśvarasūtras. Though the diacritical marks were employed here too, they were abandoned later. All consonants of the Māheśvarasūtras have inherent a.

By this time, their language was gradually moving to the next stage which is called agglutinative. Though the words were still monosyllabic, they began to add -gha for 'future' and -ga for 'injunction', as imaginable from numerous sign-pairs with these two syllables. These two are profusely illustrated. We can surmise that they had some divine warning about some future catastrophe. That is why, almost all clauses with the future affix in the verb are followed by the injunctive affix after the verb in the next clause, indicating that 'a certain event will take place; do the needful'.

Though not definitely illustrated, there was -ṭha for past, -ha for Perfect and -ra for Pluperfect also. The past affix · ṭha was dentalised and deaspirated to -ta just before the emergence of the vedic language, -ha and -ra are continuing till today in the rustic dialects, although they can also be traced to the Sanskrit forms with -maha and -cara. Most importantly, there was the prefix ā- for the past, but that also does not appear to be illustrated in the inscriptions.

It was just at this stage of the language that they faced a tragic natural catastrophe. They dispersed hopelessly, one group not knowing the fate of the others.The western group went to the land of the Soma-plants on the Iran-Afgan border; the northern group settled in the land of the seven rivers; the southern group went to the land of the hot sun (Dra-vi-ḍa); and the eastern group entered the hills and forests of central India.

It is here that the ground for the racial distinction was broken by the nature itself; geographically they were already dispersed; and linguistically a major distinction was to take place.

The western and northern groups were fortunate in having favourable conditions for their life and language. The language crossed the agglutinative stage and, ultimately, became inflexional. When they increased in population, a major group among them proceeded towards Central Asia. From here they branched into two groups which have been linguistically distinguished as satem and centum. The remaining population tilled the land and called themselves Aryans. They also composed hymns in praise of the Soma plants. But soon they had some cultural conflict among themselves and a part of them migrated to the land of the seven rivers. All the Soma-hymns of the RV, specially the 9th cycle, were composed in the land of the Soma plants where, many centuries later, the Avesta was composed. In the land of the seven rivers, the migrating Aryans saw their brethrens singing the glory of the lost urban civilisation: Agni was the officer in charge of enlightenment; Indra was the supreme commander of the armed forced, assisted by Maruts of the air-wing and Varuṇa of the navy. Rudra was in charge of the civil administration, the most strict officer to be afraid of. Viṣṇu was in charge of the land-survey. And so on. They were the real historical personages of the lost urban civilisation, who have wrongly been associated with the aspects of nature.

The life and languages of the southern and eastern groups were crippled in the unfavourable conditions of the nature. The languages were just limping forward with the wretched life of the people.

We do not know, how many thousands of years passed. A stanza of the RV (7,103,9) may lead us back to 7000 BC. The time of the composition of the other hymns of the RV may go even earlier. This was the beginning of the Vedic culture. The fire-men of the urban Indus culture, the Atri family among them, became the fire-priests; the fire-brigade of the urban culture became the rescuers, later the physicians, represented by the Aśvins (members of the rapid action force) who had rescued the Atris from the centrally heated room, later becoming abyss where fruits are matured; the steam-engineers of the urban culture became solicitors. A whole chapter can be written on this subject.

Long before the beginning of the composition of the hymns, the inflexional stage of the mother language had begun dwindling in inflexion. During the composition of the RV and AV and the later Saṃhitās much was lost and the language had made a slope down-wards. It was during the course of this decadence that Pāṇini had appeared who arrested the language from further loss.

The popular form of the language, drastically reduced in inflexion and simplified for the everyday use of the people, could not be arrested. It went on changing.

It was at this stage of the Vedic Volkssprache that the people of the 'land of the hot sun' (Dravida) and the cultivators of the north (Aryans) met by the way of cultural exchange. Agastya went to south, carrying with him the Vedic language on the one hand and the popular language on the other. The language of the land of the hot sun was still agglutinative, which appeared to match improperly with the Vedic Volkssprache, carrying with it the reflexes of the agglutinative elements, -jana in sakhi-jana for the nominative pl., adhi- in adhi-hari for the locative sg., and so on.

The south Indian languages borrowed words from the north, and the north Indian languages borrowed simple morphology from the south. Both enriched each other, the fair-skinned north Indians mingling with the dark-skinned south Indians even matrimonially, as mentioned by Kālidāsa (Ragh 6,65): indīvara-śyāma-tanur nṛpo' sau tvaṃ rocanāgaura-śarīra-yaṣṭiḥ (That king like blue lotus, and you like the white powder).

At the grass-root of the Indian society, however, from north to south and from east to west, the same undeveloped agglutinative language of the lost mother culture was still in vogue. The emperor Aśoka, a Magadhan prince educated in Taxila, in the 3rd century BC, advised his officers in charge of inscriptions to engrave his messages in the grassroot language of the society. It was neither Sanskrit nor the popular Prakrit, but the language of the grassroot society, the agglutinative Indus with the modern vocabulary. That is why, the same language appears in Gāndhāra and in Andhra of the Aśokan empire. The language of the Aśokan inscriptions is thus the common language of India at the grassroot of the society.

Pushing the language of the Aśokan inscriptions several thousand years back, we can say that the language of the Indus inscriptions is Ur-Sanskrit, which could be discovered only through linguistic Darwinism, the linguistic embryology giving scientific status to linguistics.

The Pre-Indo-European

What we call the proto-Indo-European language is the inflexional stage of Indus, marked with the gradual morphological developments, differently at different milestones on its pulsating march towards the west. It was not static and not also the same for all the dialects. If at all, it was only so on the first syllable, which was the seed.

Phonology

The original Indus syllabary, when it was finally drafted numerically (vowels and consonants kept apart), was the following:

u	i	o	e	au	ai	āu	āi		
	ẖa						ṣa	sa	śa
pa	ka	ta	ṭa	ca	tha	ṭha	kha	pha	cha
da	ḍa	ga	ba	ja	dha	ḍha	gha	bha	jha
na	ṇa	ṅa	ma	ña					
la	ra	va	ya	ha					

It was redrafted by the Sanskrit school when the language had changed typologically and the sounds of different qualities were somewhat arbitrarily arranged as regards their places of utterance. The edited Indus syllabary was called the Māheśvarasūtras (MS).

The vowel series was split into four groups, and in each case the order was reversed: i u, e o, ai au, āi āu. Besides, a, inherent in every consonant but not shown numerically in the Indus script, was placed at the beginning of the first group. Further, because e o had become obsolete and ṛ (and ḷ) had developed from ra (and la) due to accent on the neighbouring syllable, ṛ ḷ replaced the original e o. The original ai au too had contracted to e o, and āi āu to ai au. Thus the first four MS are as follows 1. a i u 2. ṛ ḷ 3. e o 4. ai au.

Pāṇini had actually apologised for beginning the vowel series with a by highlighting u (1,2,27). The signs of the Indus script no. 218 and 29 appear to be read gaī and raū, but they may probably be gāi and rāu. Although ṛ ḷ are reconstructed for IE, it was only in Vedic that ṛ developed from ra (and la); e.g. ṛtû (season) from ratu (Av. ratu 'time'), which itself goes to some original *la ṭhu (the time rolls on), as imaginable from ṛtá (the regular order of the universe) for rata from la ṭha 2124, 3083, 1268 (the time turns round).

The Indus consonantal series began with the voiceless h̲a and ended with the voiced ha. It is suggested by the fact that some numbers start from the voiceless h̲a; e.g. h̲a-p-ta = 7 and h̲a-ṣ-ṭa = 8. The h was retained in Iranian, but either lost or replaced by s in other dialects: 7 = sapta in Sanskrit, but hapta in Avesta; 8 = aṣṭa in Sanskrit, oktō in Greek, but hasht in modern Persian.

The Sanskrit school reads the consonant syllabary beginning with the voiced h. Besides, the places of ch and kh as well as of ṣa and sa were interchanged. The order of the edited MS was this: 5. ha ya va ra 6. la 7. ña ma ṅa ṇa na 8. jha bha 9. gha ḍha dha 10. ja ba ga ḍa da 11. kha pha cha ṭha tha ca ṭa ta 12. ka pa 13. śa ṣa sa 14. ha.

In Sanskrit phonology, h is only voiced, and the palatal c ch j jh are only stops, liable to interchange with velars, but in Indus they were also partly affricates. Thus 5 = pañca in Sanskrit, but pente in Greek.

Morphology

The inflexional Indus or IE has developed from the isolating stage of Indus, where there was no grammar or morphology. But there were certain rules of syntax.

There were clauses of the following types:

1. s + v: ṇa ra (creature speed) = An animal is going.

5094 ṇaga (light movement) = The light is going away.

2. s + o + v: na ma ṣa (knowledge happiness embryo) = The knowledge produces happiness.

1305

rau ci ṣa (fire light embryo) = The fire produces light.

2659, 2374, 1365, 4464

3. Oblique-case + s + v: ta na ṣa (womb gem embryo) = From the womb gems come out.

This was the normal order. It was broken for specific purposes.

4. v + obl.: gā va (movement dwelling) = Goes into the pen.

5. obl. + v: bī ja (water birth) = In the water it grows.

The subject was repeated to show plurality:

4251 rā rā rā ma the fires are exhinguished.

If the verb was repeated, it showed intensification of the verbal idea. Thus dha = shines, but dha dha = shines brightly.

The verb bhu reduplicated with bha: bha bhu.

Gradually, the clauses began to contract as phrases and, later, as lexical words: ṇara = a going animal, a man; gāva = going into the pen, cattle; rama = the extinguished fire, ashes, rāma = a black man, etc.

The agglutinative Indus

Later, the language moved towards the agglutinative stage, and the grammatical elements began to appear.

In conjugation:

-gha was added to verbs to show futurity and -ga to show injunction. There was also -tha for past: 4378 dra-gha, ra-ga (conflagration-future, speed-order)= There will be conflagration; do run away. (..........) ṣa-ṭha (be-past) = there was.

The extant Indus inscriptions do not say anything more on morphology.

Later, as inferred from Sanskrit, there was -ma for the habitual past and the prefix ā- for the general past: sa-ma (continuity-past) = continued. It contracted to s-ma and was used as postposition to turn present into past in Sanskrit: gacchati sma (goes-continued) = used to go. ā-ha (past-say) = said, ā-ṣa (past-be) = there was, ā-gā (past-go) = went.

There was -ha for Perfect: ma-ha (time-perfect) = has grown old (P. 4,2,36). There was -ra for Pluperfect: ca-ra (be-pluperfect) = had been, had taken place. (P. 5,3,53).

An agglutinative clause was like this: tata maha = The father has grown old (cf. tatā-maha 'grandfather'). The clause iti ha āṣa has been naturalised in Sanskrit as iti ha āsa 'thus, they say, it was' (also contracted as itihāsa 'a narrative'). The Vedic kucara (said to mean 'roming at will), gocara (visible) etc. are contracted Indus clauses.

In declension:

(Not attested through the Indus inscriptions)

There was -ha for dual: ṇara-ha, gāva-ha (because there are two ha sounds in Indus). There was -ṣa for pl.: ṇara-ṣa, gāva-ṣa (because there are three sibilants). There was -ti for the oblique case in general: i-ti (this-manner) = thus. There was -sa for genitive (as in Aśokan inscriptions), also extended to s-ya. There was probably -te for ablative and -si for locative sg. (as in Aśokan inscriptions). As inferred from the later phase of the language, there was -ma for object to distinguish it from subject in sg.: ṇara-ma, gāva-ma.

Because just at the beginning of the agglutinative stage of the language, the Indus community had dispersed, the morphology began to differ from group to group. All the dialects became widely or narrowly divergent due to developing their own affix elements.

When the plurality was shown in the subject, even the verb was correspondingly modified. Here the sg. form of the verb was bent towards u before taking the plural ending -ṣa:

ā-ha: āhu-ṣa

ā-ṣa: āṣu-ṣa

ā-gā: āgu-ṣa

The reduplicated verb was similarly turned into pl.:

dha-dha: dhadhu-ṣa

In case of bhu, -va was added to the sg. form before which the final u was lenghtened: bhabhū-va. Then this sg. form was bent towards u before the pl. suffix: bhabhūvu-ṣa.

Even the sg. dhadha was later extended as dhadhā-u.

At the advanced agglutinative stage, it became necessary to distinguish 'persons', at least in sg. There was -ta for 3rd person, -sa for second person, and -ma for 1st person:

3. ā-gā-ta

2. ā-gā-sa

1. ā-gā-ma

Later the prefix was shortened to a: a-gā-ta, etc.

The present forms were conceived by slightly bending the endings towards i:

3. gā-ti
2. gā-si
1. gā-mi

To express order, the affix was bent toward u in 3rd person:

gā-tu yā-tu

In 2nd person, the affix was -dhi (later also -hi):

ga-dhi ga-hi

The verbs were also turned into pl. by interposing -n- in 3rd person: yā-ti: yā-n-ti, yā-tu: yā-n-tu

In 2nd person, there was -tha for present in pl.:

yā-si: yā-tha

In 1st person, the past affix ma itself was extended by -si for pl. in present:

yā-mi: yā-masi

To express order, there was -ta in pl.

yā-hi: yā-ta

The language was evolving and developing in uneven way. One form used to influence the other, and gradually the whole system was regularised.

The reduplicated verbs generally gave birth to the perfect system, but partially also appeared in the present system of Vedic

	Perfect		Present	
3.	dhadhā-u	dhadhu-ṣa	dhadhā-ti	dhadha-ti
2.			dhadhā-si	
1.			dhadhā-mi	

When dhadha-ti was conceived as pl., the sg., forms were conceived by lengthening the base.

At the agglutinative stage itself, the monosyllabic verbs were extended by specific syllables: ja-ya, ka-ra, bha-va, ha-va, ga-ma, va-da, ra-bha, dha-gha, etc. The extension by cha was very remarkable: ra-cha, pra-cha, ga-cha, i-cha, etc.

From the vocable tánas, at the inflexional stage, the verb tan was deduced, which was responsible for the various groupings of the verbs: It was extended by -o (tan-o-ti), and it gave birth to tan-class in Vedic; its -no- was added to a number of verbs, which form the su-class (su-no-ti) in vedic; its -nā- (from *tan-ā-ti) gave birth to kri-class (jān-ā-ti, cf. Persian mī-dān-am) in Vedic; its -na, n- (in *tan-a-ti) gave birth to rudh-class (ru-na-d-dhi, ru-n-dh-anti) in Vedic.

The IE language

This was the background of the IE language. This pre-IE was still monotonous, but ultimately it became accented, followed by remarkable events, differently in different dialects.

The Dravidian and Santhal groups of languages, as well as other pockets in the heartland, however, marked time on the agglutinative stage, thanks to the unfavourable conditions in those regions. But other dialects show the developments as briefly described below. The language reached its youth or reproductive age, when it could multiply as needed.

1. The forms began to expand but differently in different languages:

bhabhu	Skt. babhū-va
	Gk. pephu-ka

2. There was a tendency for deaspiration at the first syllable:

bhabhū-va : babhū-va
dhadhā-u : dadhau

3. There was a tendency for devoicing in specific dialects:

bhu Gk. : pephu-ka
dha : tithemi

4. There was a tendency for dentalisation:

Skt. ṭha : ta
ḍha : dha

In Dravidian the cerebrals were generally retained. But as the language left the home-land and proceeded towards the west, the cerebrals were wiped out.

5. There was a tendency for the lengthening of the final vowels before nasals and semivowels:

bhabhu : babhū-va (but cf. ad-bhuta)
bhava : bhavā-mi

6. The accent reduced the size of forms in Sanskrit:

ā-ha : āḥ
ā-ṣa : ās RV. 10, 129, 3 b
gāva-ṣa : gā́vas
ṇara-ṣa : nárás

A large number of Vedic words are the reduced forms of the Indus clauses and phrases:

rama (extinguished fire): rám (ash) RV 2,4,5c
4225 mana (shining gem): mán (ornament) RV 8,78,2
5094 naga (going light): nág (night) RV 7,71,1
tanasa (a gem from the womb): tánas (offspring) RV 5,70,4

7. The voiceless h suffered different changes in different languages:

hapta : Skt. sapta, Av. hapta
haṣṭa : aṣṭa, Gk, oktō̄, mod. Persian hasht

8. The original a also was twisted towards e and o as the

language proceeded towards the west.

9. There was the birth of ṛ ḷ from ra la in Vedic on account of accent on the neighbouring syllable:

rachati : ṛcháti
prachati : pṛcháti
la ṭha (ra ta) : ṛtá

In Gk ch was replaced by sk(h), in Latin by sc, and so on.

10. The Indus h-sounds were reduced to just voiced h in Vedic, but survived in Hittite as the voiced and voiceless laryngeals. The uncontractableness of the final ī and ū of the Sanskrit duals is due to this lost h (kavi-ha ripu-ha > kavi-H ripu-H > kavī ripū). The duals in ā are also due to this: gāva-ha > gāvaH > gāvā. In other IE dialects, the original h was lost but h arose again from other sources.

The first wave of the Indus Aryans settled in Central Asia, and then they marched ahead divided as Centum and Satem groups.

The IE etymological dictionary

The extant IE etymological dictionaries have to be revised. The cognate words should begin with the first sound.

ẖa 'horse' (Indus): + śa 'injury' + va 'strength' = ẖa-ś-va Vedic á-śva (injuriously strong); + ra (speed) + va = ẖa-r-va Vedic arvā (fast and strong); prefixed with gand- (= gard in garda-bha 'ass') = gandharva 'an assed horse' (a new breed); + śa-pha (hoof) = ẖa-ś-pha Av. aspa 'a horse with injurious hoofs'; + ka-va = ẖakva Lat. equus; + pa-va = ẖapva Gk. hippos + r + sa = hors in Germanic.

As ẖa reached different countries, special qualities began

to be attached to the simple horse, also as its breed was improved. Later, when aś was conceived as a verb 'to run fast, be quick', even ś-van (dog) was derived from it, the radical a lost due to accent on the suffix.

vra (va 'strong' + ra 'fire'). It was extended by -ka in Vedic, > vṛka (strong and furious) 'wolf'; reduced to lu- in Gk and Latin before taking -ko and -pu respectively; dissolved as vil- before taking -ka in Lithuanian (vilka), as vol- before taking -p in Germanic (Eng. wolf).

etc.

The IE dictionary should be realistic. It should not be a tower of Babel.

The Reduplicated Verbal Forms

The syllables signifying verbs were reduplicated to intensify the verbal idea at the isolating stage of Indus; e.g. dha dha (shines brightly), etc. At the agglutinative stage, when the plural was desired to be expressed, the final a was bent towards u before the pl. affix -ṣa ; e.g. dha dha: dha dhu-ṣa.

When the 'person' began to be distinguished, -ti was added in the 3rd person: dha dha-ti. This form was, anyhow, conceived to be pl. Then the corresponding sg. form was conceived by lengthening the preceding vowel in all persons: 3. dha dhā-ti 2. dha dhā-si 1 dha dhā-mi.

Later, the sg. form corresponding to the pl. dha dhu-ṣa was extended by -u, also lengthening the base: dha dhā-u.

Thus, gradually, two sets of reduplicated present forms emerged in the language:

3. dhadhā-u	dhadhu-ṣa	and	3. dhadhā-ti	dhadha-ti
2. —	—		2. dhadhā-si	—
1. —	—		1. dhadhā-mi	—

Other forms emerged later.

The verb bha was reduplicated with bhu: bha bhu. Later it was extended by -va in the 3p., the base being lenghened: bhabhūva. Before adding the pl. affix -ṣa, the sg. form was bent towards u: bha bhū vu-ṣa.

With this small legacy the agglutinative Indus transited into the inflexional stage, and then there was a wonderful spring for the new flowers of forms. The reduplicated class in the present system and the Perfect system arose simultaneously.

The major events at the inflexional stage were:

(i) the rise of accent, due to which the size of the verbal forms are reduced.

(ii) the deaspiration at the first syllable.

Thus the corresponding inflexional forms were the following:

dádhā-ti	dadhati	
dádhā-si	dhat-ta	for *dadh-ta (the aspiration thorwn back on the first syllable).
dádhā-mi	dadh-ma	
	and	
babhū-va	babhūv-us	

The Vedic verbal form pibati (he drinks) is controversial as to its origin from the root pā (to drink).

The Sanskrit lexicon of the monosyllabic words ascribes 'water' as one of the meanings of ba. As a verb, it may mean 'to drink'. At the isolating Indus stage, its reduplicated form ba-ba should have meant 'drinks repeatedly'. At the agglutinative stage, when the 'persons' were required to be distinguished, a form like *biba-ti would have emerged. At the inflexional stage, the first syllable would have been devoiced: pi-ba-ti.

As a parallel case, we may conceive tudati (afflicts). The verb du (dunoti) also means 'to afflict'. The reduplicated du-du would have emerged as du-da-ti at a late agglunative stage, from which we could have tudati at the inflexional stage.

Texts

The texts of the extant Indus inscriptions mainly represent the language of the isolating stage, that is, a language having no grammar or morphology. But when the writing had started, the language had already made a move towards the next, that is, the agglutinative stage.

In the present collection of texts, the purely isolating stage is presented first (A), then the agglutinative stage (B). In the middle, there is also a transitional stage: there is no affix element, but there is some trick to change the idea or to connect two clauses in the same line. If the second clause has ṣa, the first clause has ṣu.

(A)

The Isolating Indus

The following are the texts of the isolating stage of the language, and only those texts are presented which are supposedly properly understood.

ṇa ga (light movement)
= The light is going away.

It is a clause with subject and verb. When the verb conceptually merged with the subject to qualify it with the same body of syllables, it became a phrase: the vanishing light. After remaining a bisyllabic word for some time, the accent on the first syllable at the inflexional stage caused the loss of the final a. It resulted as nág, meaning 'night', and is attested through a single occurrence in the RV (7, 71,

1)* Here it appears, as if the word nág is again expanded to its Indus size: apa svasur uṣaso nág jihīte = The night is running away from its sister 'dawn'.

 ṣa ṭha (embryo circle)
= The ball rolled

This is the meaning what a common man can say. But it certainly refers to "the glowing cloud millions of miles in diameter blossoming out in space" which they somehow knew from their primitive ancestors. By the time they had come to write these messages they had achieved wonderful advance in science and technology.

At the phrase stage, both the syllables were dentalised and the final th was also deaspirted. The bisyllabic phrase *sata further lost the final a due to accent on the first syllable at the inflexional stage. In the RV, sát (the rolling ball) occurs several times. Even at that time it was as heavy as a clause, and it was again expanded in the inflexional Vedic with the same meaning: hiraṇya-garbhaḥ sam-avartatāgre = A golden embryo rolled forth (RV. 10, 121,1). We can now imagine that those primitive people did not mean anything

---

* It is difficult to present a comparative decipherment and interpretation of the texts of the Indus inscriptions. The interpretation would have been comparable if the reading would have matched syllabically. But 'a number of signs representing the same sound and the same sign representing a number of sounds' offer only slippery ground for comparison. An interpretation based on syllabic reading may match with the logoraphic interpretation, but the latter changes ground every now and then like the shadow of the cloud. Moreover, it is generally purely subjective and cannot reveal the intention of the original writer, unless it is the universally accepted logograph like +, –, =, etc.

Therefore, any attempt for comparison has been at least postpned, if not cancelled at all.

else by ṣa ṭha. It appears that they were describing to their younger generation how the world came into being. They were as wise men as we think ourselves to be.

Unfortunately, at the Vedic stage itself, there was the birth of the present participle sát from the root as 'to be' which, though sant in the strong forms, was sat in the weak forms, the accent then shifting on the endings, and was confused with the primitive sat. Though the ṛṣis of the RV could distinguish them, at least in the strong forms, later there was unsoluble confusion. Ultimately, the homonym sát tilted in favour of the participal meaning, and the 'rolling embryo' was totally forgotten.

Though the teachers of the early Upaniṣads had still some idea of the 'rolling embryo' (sad eva somyedam agra āsīt Chānd. Up. 6, 2, 1), the younger Upaniṣads replaced this sat with ātman (Ait. up 1, 1, 1). The commentators of the Upaniṣads did not conceive anything beyond the participal meaning, and the same has continued upto Sāyaṇa, Roth Macdonell and Geldner.

It is clear, the Indus text ṣa ṭha has marched along the different phases of the language, and even when it was reduced to sát at the inflexional vedic stage, it was as heavy as the isolating clause. Therefore, it was explained by the ṛṣi-kavis with a new but exact paraphrasing, word for word. However there are certain other Indus texts which have not marched along the different phases of the language but which have direct paraphrasing in the RV.

The following text has two lines:

ci ha̱ ba ba ta gra ṣa

śa da bha ṇa ṣa-gha

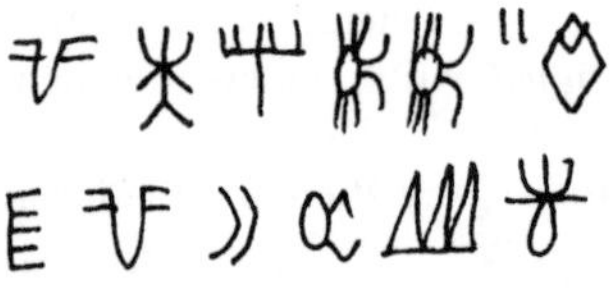

truth say water water womb sun be
strength heat light knowledge embryo-future

The first line seems to say:"truly speaking, (there was) water everywhere; in the womb the sun there was". This reflects in the RV (10,129,3b): apraketaṃ salilaṃ sarvam ā idam (Indistinguishable all this was water).

In the present context, ta gra ṣa has an entirely different meaning ." The sun was there in the womb" indicates complete darkness, which has been paraphrased by apraketam.

The second line seems to say: " from the strongly hot light intelligence will come out." This seems to reflect in 3d of the same stanza: tapasas tan mahinājāyataikam (That one arose through the power of heat).

The Indus syllabic group da bha itself appears as tap 'to be hot' in devoiced and deaspirated form. It is also interesting to note that what the Indus text says in future is rendered in Vedic by past form, Naturally, the Indus culture was past by the Vedic period.

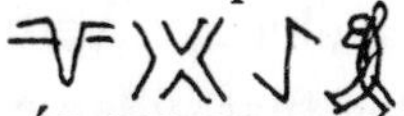

śa ma yo ṣa (evil end comfort embryo)
= Let evil come to an end; let comfort be there.

Obviously, there are two clauses, and they express the will of the speaker. As a rule, they could also express present, past or future, because the tense or the mood could be known from the context at the isolating stage.

At the agglutinative stage they could have become phrases with the same body of syllables, and śama actually occurs in Sanskrit carrying the idea of the clause. From this word itself the verb śám 'to be pacified' has evolved. Even yo ṣa occurs separately in the texts, where it seems to mean 'gives comfort'. Perhaps, it has evolved as yóṣā (wife) in Sanskrit, originally meaning 'giving comfort'. Thus both śa ma and yo ṣa have transited with their original forms in Sanskrit.

But, otherwise, at the inflexional stage, due to accent on the first syllable, the final a in both cases was lost . They appear as śám yós together and sometimes with ca (śáṃ ca yóśca).*

Later, though śam could survive as the first member of some compounds (śaṅkara, śambhu), yós could not go beyond the RV. It should be noted that the syllable śa had originally a bad and injurious sense. It was in the company of ma that it acquired a good sense:

But perhaps the secondary suffix - yu (in mitra-yu, etc.) is the reduced form of yós (cf. P.3,1,8 and 3,2,70).

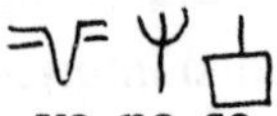

va ṇa ṣa (water life embryo)
= The water gives life.

This clause consists of the subject + object + verb. At the inflexional stage, due to accent on the first syllable, the final a was lost and vánas (plant) became a lexical word. It forms the first member of the compound vánas-páti (plants in general). Its shorter form vana (wood)survives in Sanskrit, but its further reduced form van is restricted to the RV (in gen. pl. van-ām and loc. pl. vaṃ.-su).

The word vánas was further reduced to varṣ, a verb meaning 'to rain' and having many derivatives.

---

* Egbert Richter interpreting it logographically as 'Soma, the king of plants, may be benevolent to our town' has been noticed earlier. Both the interpretations are widely apart.

It is also said to mean 'loveliness, beauty' and ' desire' in other contexts. The root derived from vánas too is said to have a number of meanings.

The bases of this fossilised word, specifically va and ṇa have a number of meanings.:

Va: air, water, dwelling, arrow, strong.

ṇa: knowledge (light), certainty (determination), ornament, bad man (evil).

These meanings are just symbolic. They may refer to other ideas, and the combined meaning may go to any direction. The clause va ṇa ṣa may also mean: 1. In the dwelling there is light; 2. On the body there is ornament; etc.

We have found a number of coins in the ruins of the Indus inscriptions. Even then we are wandering in the desolate deserts.

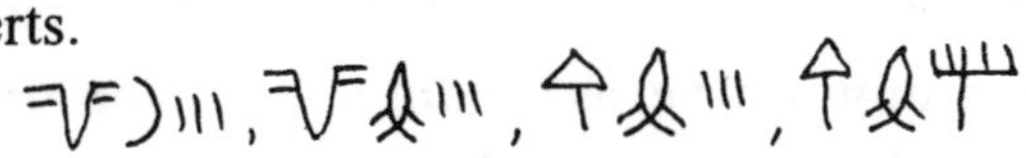

ta na ṣa (womb gem embryo)
From the womb gems come out.

This is a clause in four graphic forms with the oblique case at the first place, followed by s + v. At the inflexional stage, it was reduced to tánas (offspring), because the gem coming out of the womb of a woman may be the child itself. We can imagine the mental and cultural standard of those primitive people.

From this tánas, the verb tan 'to expand ' was deduced, because the family expands due to the offspring. This verb tan was used in variously extended forms:

1. It was extended as tan - o - before the endings distinguishing ' persons' in sg. (3. Tano-ti 2. Tano-ṣi 1. Tano-mi). Some three or four verbs ending with n formed similar

bases, and this group of verbs was known as tan-class in the Vedic grammar.

2. The -no- part of tan -o- was attached to some other group of verbs (3. Su-no-ti 2. Su-no-ṣi 1. Su-no-mi), and it was known as su-class.

3. It was also extended as *tan -ā̃-, but this base itself could not endure. On the other hand, its -nā̃- was attached to another group of verbs (3.pu-nā-ti 2. Pu-nā -si 1. Pu-nā-mi), which was known as krī-class. The analogy of* tan-ā̃ was, however, followed by another Indus verb jān (3.jān-ā--ti, etc.) which, with the affricate value dz of /j/, appears as dān- in Old Persian and zān- in Avesta. The verb jān itself was contracted as jñā- in the Vedic language .Thus the Vedic jā-nā-ti is actually jān-ā-ti rather than jñā + nā +ti.

4. It had also an imaginary base* tan-a-, and its -na-was put inside a group of verbs ending with consonants (3.yu-na-k-ti 2. Yu-na-k-ṣi 1. Yu-na-j-mi from yuj), which was reduced to -ṇ- in weak forms (3. Yu-ṅ-k-tas yu-ñ-j-anti, etc.).

Thus this tan alone was responsible for the development of four classes of verbs in the present system of verbs in the Vedic grammar.

We can evaluate Kuiper's Indogermanishe nasal presentia in this connection.

Even the vocable tánas was further reduced to the verb tarṣ 'to be thirsty', because the desire for an offspring is a kind of thirst. In Gothic, it appears as Thars. We will see later, the past form of the clause ta na ṣa, namely ta na ṣa-ṭha, has apppeared in the Germanic languages (Eng. thirst, Germ. durst). This tarṣ has certain derivatives in Sanskrit, but all of them die by the end of the middle Indic.

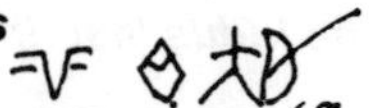

rau ci ṣa (fire light embryo)
= From the fire there is light.

Because there is rócis (light) in Sanskrit, this text has been provisionally read as above, but it appears that this reading and interpretation is correct.

From rocis the root ruc' to shine' was deduced, which has a number of derivatives with varying meanings. When the initial r changed into l, the verb loc 'to see' and its derivatives loc-ana (eye), etc. developed.

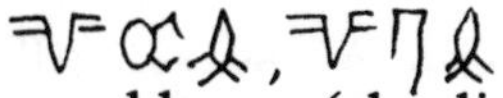

na bha ṣa (sky light embryo)
= In the sky there is light.

This clause was reduced to nábhas (sky) at the inflexional stage, which has a number of other meanings. It is only the main idea which surivies when the clause is reduced to a lexical word.

In the later phase of the language, almost on the threshold of the inflexional stage, the initial n was lost and the second syllable was devoiced as well as deaspirated. Thus ap 'water' appears in its latest form (āp-as, ap-as, ap-ām, ap-su), the final p also dissimilated as d before the middle endings with bh (adbhis, etc.).

Even napāt may be connected with this source.

va ṇa ra (dwelling life speed)
= In the dwelling the creatures go.
= The dwelling gives safety.

This clause was reduced to vanar at the inflexional stage, forming the first part of the compounds vanar-gu and vanar-ṣad in the RV. This vanar finds no place in the Vedic lexicography, because vánas was already there, inspite of the phonetic difficulty, to misguide the scholars. This word did not survive beyond the RV, because it was already very old by that time.

This word retains the meaning of the first syllable of the clause of the isolating stage, but it varies for individual cases: 'nest' for the birds,'altar' for the fire, a 'den' for the robbers and a 'stable' for the cows.

It is perhaps in vanar that we find the real base of what later developed as vānar-a (monkey), which is variously conceived as vā-nara (looking like a man) or vana + ra =vāna-ra (living in the forest).

It appears that vānara originally referred to 'cavemen' and nar to 'creatures' in general (RV 7,103,9: náras), but when later nar (nara) was restricted for 'human beings', vānara shifted to 'monkeys', because by that time the 'cavemen' had disappeared or moved to towns and villages.

va ṭho ṣa (dwelling disc embryo)
= From the dwelling the disc comes out.

The clause simply means to say that 'the foetus comes out of the womb'. At the inflexional stage, it has emerged as vatsá. Due to accent on the last syllable, the vowel of the central syllable has been lost, the consonant itself dentalised and deaspirated, as in many other cases, the most notable among them being the Vedic past affix - ta.

Later, the consonant-cluster -ts- in vatsa became an affricate -ch- in Prakrit. Not only an affricate splits as a consonant- cluster, even the latter becomes an affricate. Thus the Indus *saci appears as haśi (through satśi) in

Avesta. Its Vedic counterpart sakhi is full of phonetic difficulty. For the Vedic aham, OP adam Av. Azem, we have to assume an Indus* ajha, /jh/with an affricate value /dzh/, elsewhere being a pure stop gh (for the Gk. Lat. Ego).

ī ka ṣa (eye joy embryo)
= The eyes give joy.

The clause contracted as the lexeme* īkṣa at the inflexional stage, form which the verb īkṣ (to see) was deduced.

Graphically, here, we have a good example of how long vowels were drawn in the primitive cryptography. If  is for i, its doubling from two sides makes ī. Similarly, for ū we can have 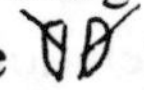 from  u in 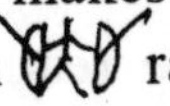 rāu or raū. It is on this ground that we take  for some vowel, probably o, added from two sides of the consonant ẖa in  for ho or hao. Also  is similarly a vowel, because it has been added to  ra from two sides in  rē or raē or what?

It is on the basis of the identity of the two texts above that 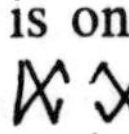 =  has been conceived as ī, made form the simple  i. But there is no clue for :

These texts have also shown that  and  are duplicates for ka.

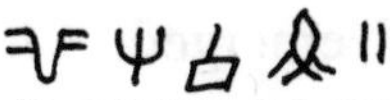

ta na va ṇa ṣa (womb gem water life embryo)

This text seems to be a combination of two clauses: ta na ṣa + va ṇa ṣa. We know what these two clauses mean. But here the first two syllables of each clause appear to have turned into phrases:

Ta na (gem form the womb) va ṇa (life through the water). These phrases too seem to have gone over to the lexical stage: tana = child, vaṇa = plant. The text now means: A child is a plant.

Just as plants grow and turn into a wood, the child causes the family to expand.

Not only the changing script but also the different phases of the isolating stage show that the writing of the inscriptions is an activity spreading over several centuries, during which one form of the script and one phase of the language dominated the other.

ca gra ṣa (eye sun embryo)
= From the eye the sun was born.

This text, if the reading and interpretation is correct, reflects in the RV (10,90,13,b): cakṣoḥ suryo ajāyata (from the eyes of the Puruṣa the sun was born).

The first two syllables of this clause have contracted as cakra (wheel), which was imaginable through the rolling ball of the sun. The central syllable gra has emerged as gl- at the beginning of many words of 'light' in the Germanic languages.

h̲a ṭha ṣa (empty-space disc embryo)
= From the empty space a ball emerged.

The voiceless ha of Indus has generally emerged as s in Sanskrit, as we can guess form h̲a-p-ta becoming sapta in Vedic but remaining hapta in Avesta. However, in h̲a-ṣ-ṭa, h is lost probably due to the following spirant, becoming aṣṭa in Vedic but remaining hašta in Iranian as suggested by the modern Persian hasht.

In the traditional Sanskrit lexicon of the monosyllabic words ha means 'sky', because the distinction between the voiceless and voiced h was lost by that time. On the other hand, a voiceless h was a fault in the eyes of the phoneticians of the RV-Prātiśākhya.

We have also seen that ṭha has become ta in Vedic. Thus the clause has naturally abbreviated as satás, which forms the first member of the following compounds: sató-bṛhat, sató- mahat and satóvira. What may be 'big', 'great' and 'strong' is perhaps the 'ball' of the universe.*)

It is only the second members of the compounds, -bṛhat (big). -mahat (great) and - vīra (strong), which somehow suggest that satás is something big, great and strong, namely the 'ball' of the universe, the hiraṇya-garbha (the golden embryo).

It is time to take the Vedas to the ruins of the Sarasvatī civilisation to find the seeds: satás = h̲a ṭha ṣa.

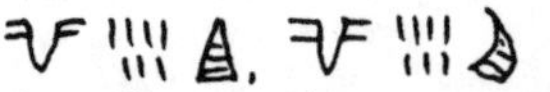

h̲a ḍha ṣa (empty-space sound embryo)
= In the empty space there was a big bang.

The first two syllables have evolved as sadha, as we find in sadha-stha. sadha-mād, etc. Thus sadha is some abode in

---

*) The meaning of satás is sharply disputed among the Vedic shcolars. Sāyaṇa, following Yāska (Nir. 3,20) seems to conceive the meaning prāpta, probably connecting it with the verb san 'to get', while Roth, followed by Geldner, takes it to be an adverb 'equally', perhaps analysing it as sa (= samāna 'equal') -tas. However, this nestor of the Vedic words, with the body already decayed beyond recognition and the breath just going in and coming out, was about to leave the scene for ever, when it was arrested by the ṛvedic singers.

the empty space, to be conceived as heaven', making the duality sadhe with the earth.*)

In the Vedic lexicography, sadha is wrongly said to be the older form of the particle saha 'with'.

) The shorter text ha ḍha, a phrase (the sound in the empty space), not attested, may be assumed to be present in the Indus language, having also a cognate form ha ḍhi, attested through the Vedic sadhi: apsv agne sadhis tava (0 Agni, you have an abode in the waters) RV 8,43,9. That is to say, though the fire and the water are opposed to each other, the former dwells in the latter.

rāu ka ṣa (fire light embryo)
= From the fire light comes.

The clause seems to have contracted as rókas (the appearance of light) in the RV (6, 66, 6). From its isolated occurrence it is not clear whether it was roka or rokas. But now it is definitely rokas.

The verb lok 'to see' has been deduced from this rare Vedic vocable, which is used with various prepositions, bases: loka-, lokaya-.

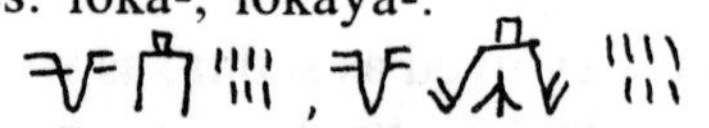

ḍha bu ṣa (frog water embryo)
= The frogs bring rain.

The reading is as doubtful as the meaning, specially at the central syllable. Both are here mainly based on a colloquial Hindi word ḍhābus, which refers to the frogs appearing at the beginning of the rainy season.

From many examples it has become clear that the Indus

a was an open vowel. While it became a 'closed vowel' by the time of Pāṇini, it is always represented by ā in the rustic dielects.

dha na ṣa (wealth gem embryo)
= The wealth causes arrogance.

Though the contracted form of this clause, namely dhanas, is not attested in the vedic language, its further reduced form dharṣ 'to be bold or arrogant' is there in Sanskrit with some derivatives. The first two syllables of this clause themselves, namely dhana, stand for wealth, though perhaps secondarily, originally meaning 'the shining gem'.

The text may also mean: the wealth earns gems, just as we generally say: money begets money.

la ṭha (time circle)
= The time turns round.

The meaning 'time 'has been given to la on the basis of Pāṇini who conceives the whole range of 'time ' under la.

We already know that the Indus ṭha was gradually dentalised and deaspirated to ta by the time of the Vedic language.

Here in la ṭha, even la has undergone rhotacism, and some proto-Vedic* rata evolved as ṛtá due to accent on the last syllable. We know that the Av. Ratu (time) appears as ṛtû in Vedic.

In the RV, ṛtá is the 'regular order' of the nature or the universe, which had developed innumerable shades of meanings in the later phase of the language. In this sense, ṛtú has more specific meanings and is restricted to the time concept alone.

For the Vedic ṛtú (season, Av ratu time) we expect la ṭhu (time circle = the time rotates), but that is not attested in the Indus texts.

The gradual change of the Indus ṭha to ta by the time of the Vedic language is liable to be questioned by a skeptic and, though the change of the articulatory position is confirmed by the RV Prātiśākhya, the deaspiration is open to question. But the Indus ṭha is definitely represented by the Vedic ta.

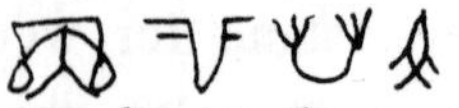

na ka ṣa ṭha

sky head heaven disc

From the highest head the heaven rolled forth.

Though na stands for the sky, finguratively it means ' the highest'. This text reflects in the RV (10,127,14 b):

śīrṣṇo dyauḥ sam-avartata

"From the head the heaven rolled forth".

If the final syllable ṭha is a past affix, sa-ṭha (be-past) = (there) was may be the finite verb with ka as its subject and na in oblique case.

Then the clause 'from/in na there was ka' may force us to wander recklessly:

from gem there was light.
in heaven there was joy.
in the sky there was light.

It could also mean: continuous (na) light (ka) there was (ṣa-ṭha).

Because -s- between two stops is lost in Vedic, the text may have been reduced to naksta and then, by the loss of

-s-, to nakta (night). which is conceived as starlit and bright. The first part of nakṣatra is not different from nakta.

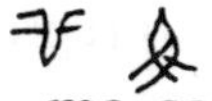

1254 ma ṣa

The clause ma ṣa seems to have fossilised as mas in Vedic, which forms the second member of the compound candra-mas (moon), nom. Sg. Candra-mās. Because candra itself means 'shining' (candrā āpas 'the shining waters'), candra-mas would have initially meant 'the shining moon'. But, at the clause stage, ma ṣa itself certainly meant: the moon is shining. At the phrase stage masa would have meant 'the shining moon'. When it was reduced to mas due to the accent. the accompanying adjective 'shining' also disappeared. But to bring the adjective back to 'moon', mas was reinforced by candra-(shining), but ultimately candra-mas also lost the accompanying adjective 'shining' and now candra-mas = moon.

4225 ma ṇa

Without going to the meaning of the text ma ṇa, we may suppose that it may have been reduced to *man at the Vedic stage. As a matter of fact, this word is not recorded in any extant Vedic dictionary. However, a Ṛgvedic stanza (8,78,2) reads thus:

ā no bhara vyañjanam
gām aṣvam abhyañjanam,
sacā manā hiraṇyayā.

For Geldner, both vyañjanam and manā are uncertain. He also seems to question Roth who has taken manā to be the basic form. The following instrumental form hiraṇyayā seems to qualify manā, which then may be the instrumental sg. form of man f. The accent has shifted to the ending in the weak case. Thus our man seems to represent the Indus clause ma ṇa in a solitary occurrence.

Because this man is said to be golden. and even maṇi (jewel) is said to be golden elsewhere (RV 1,33,8. AV 12,1,44), our man is not different from maṇi While the Indus clause *ma ni could remain intact in course of transmission, ma ṇa was reduced to man. The clause ma ṇa means: the moon shines Then man is gem or ornament which shines like the moon.

The vedic ṛṣi, on his part, wants his house to be filled with various ointments, cattle, horses, and golden ornaments.

4289 ra na ṣa

This text occurs several times in the extant Indus inscriptions. Obviously, its fossilised form in Vedic may be * ranas, which is unattested. But its reduced form ran occurs only once (RV 1,120,7), taken by Sāyaṇa to be the agentive present participle of rā (to give) = dātārau. On the other hand, Geldner takes it to mean 'joy' from ram to rejoice as an object of āstam. In a straightforward manner, maho ran (in the predicate) should be in apposition to yuvam (the subject): yuvam = yuvām maho ran āstam (You two were the great producer of wealth). The vocable ran was originally raṇas qualified by mahas. Towards the beginning of the Vedic language, when the original raṇas was reduced to ran as vánas to van, the particle hi was brought to save the metre. That is to say, yuvam āstam maho raṇas (prosodially a better reading) was replaced by 'yuvaṃ hi āstaṃ maho ran', not only disturbing the metre but also making the verse obscure.

If ran is the reduced form of *ránas, the clause ra na sa may be understood thus: the fire produces gems. This is the seed idea. The RV (1,1,3) paraphrases it in the following way: agninā rayim aśnavat (through Agni one may get wealth).

We may be tempted to say that some Ṛgvedic stanzas belong to the inflexional Indus, which were redrafted by the Vedic ṛṣis when the language underwent further reduction in some vocables.

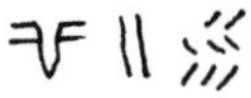

4094 ṣa ra ṣa

The text ṣa ra ṣa may be supposed to have fossilised as saras (pond, lake, sea) in the RV. One of the meanings of ṣa is nipple' which may refer to the 'source of the waters' e.g. the mountain. Then it may be in the ablative case. The syllable ra (speed) may indicate the flowing of waters, and ṣa (end) may indicate the stop. Thus saras (lake, sea) might have been so called because the waters flowing from the mountain stopped here. The clause ṣa ra ṣa thus means: From the mountains (the waters)flow (and)stop (on the way).

The river Sarasvatī was so called because it had hundreds of ponds throughout the bed from its place of orgin to the place where it disappeared.During the rainy season the ponds were connected by the flow from the mountain.After the rainy season, the river ceased to flow but ponds were distinctly visible which gave it the name saras-vat-ī (abounding in saras).

If the natural ponds or small lakes starting from the foot of the Himalayas towards the sea, parallel to the beds of the rivers Gaṅgā and Yamunā as well as Sindhu are marked on the map, the bed of the river Sarasvatī can be reconstructed. Now it is said not to have merged with Gaṅgā and Yamunā at Prayāga but to have descended in the Arabean sea.

The river Sarasvatī was flowing mightily during the period of the composition of the RV. Very excellent academic activities had started on the two banks of the river, and it appeared that the learning flowed with the stream of this river. Other rivers, Sindhu in the west and Gaṅgā in the east just lay on the periphery, although there too the centres of learning had started working .

When the river Sarasvatī dried up by 1900 BC, it was deified, and the name Sarasvatī became the goddess of learning. By that time, the whole Vedic literature had become an old document.

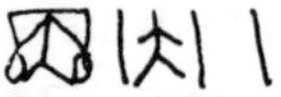

la rā ṭha

If the above text correctly reads la rā ṭha, that may have a shadow in the Vedic rarāṭa (VS 5, 21.24,1), later also lalāṭa 'forehead'. Perhaps la (time) ra (fire) ṭha (disc) means: in ancient times the fire was carried around. The early graphic form of ṭha portrays a bearer . The fire was carried from house to house for kindling in the evening, and it was put near the forehead, which became the point of reference.

h̲a dha bha

The last two syllables dha bha reflect in the Vedic dabh (to injure, deceive) and its derivatives . The initial aspiration has been lost, but it has been restored in the desiderative dhips while in dab-dha it has shifted to the suffix. The same dha bha may have also appeared as the devoiced and deaspirated tap (to be hot) as well as dhūp (sunlight) and the colloquial dhīp (to be hot). The injurious and the sublime aspects of the heat and the light seem to centre round this group.

The first syllable h̲a meaning 'the empty space' may be in some oblique case. The syllable ḍha stands for the heat of the sun, and bha points to brightness, appearance. Now the clause h̲a dha bha may be said to mean: in the empty space the sun appeared.

Corresponding to dha bha, there is also dha gha (bright sun) which we find in ni-dāgha (summer), Eng. Day, Germ. Tag, etc. The 'day' (dha-gha)is so called because the bright sun makes it hot. Its devoiced and deaspirated form *taka appears in some doubtful Vedic words (taku, tak-man, tak-va, tak-van, etc.). They appear to be connected with heat and light in meaning. The same syllabic group dha gha has also other meanings as imagined from uru-dagh-na (reaching thigh) and Hindi postposition tak (upto).

The same /dh/and /gh/ phonemes make another pair dhu gha with a changed vowel at the first syllable followed by a difinite change in the meaning. At the isolating stage, dhu gha could mean: the liquid shines. At the agglutinative stage, it would have been a phrase: the shining liquid. The devoiced and deaspirated form of dhugha may be * tuka which we find in the Vedic toka (child) and the Persian tokhm (seed). The phrase dhugha made another clause with tara, meaning 'emits shining liquid', and dhugh-tara has fossilised as thugater in Greek and * duhítar in Indic. Though the accent has shifted to the suffix in Vedic (duhitár), Pali dhitā shows the result of the original accent. Probably, duhitar was so called because she 'produced children'.

We also imagine other groups like dhe gha, gha dha and gha bha, which reflect in many Vedic words. The group bha gha (bright sun) reflects in the Vedic bhaga, said to refer to the time 'after-noon ' when the sun is brightly hot. The Vedic root bhaj and its devoiced and deaspirated form pac has a wide range of meanings connected with 'heat'.

The Vedic Sabda

If the order of the second and third signs of the text cited above is changed, the resulting h̲a bha dha seems to have fossiblised as sabda, which is semantically obscure in the following two occurrences:

> sábdaḥ sagaraḥ sumekaḥ TS 4,4,7,2.
> sábdam ahah sagarā rātriḥ SB 1,7,2,26.

All the words of the first text are adjectives. But in the second text, sabdam qualifies ahan n (day) and sagara qualifies rātrī f (night). Naturally, we are likely to conceive sabda as 'bright' and sagara as 'dark'.

But at least for the singers of the RV, rātrī (with the long vowel ī, being rā-tṛ + ī ' illuminator') is not conceived as the dark, but the bright starlit night (Macdonell, Vedic Reader,p.203). Therefore, sagara must have some different meaning.

If sabda means 'bright' and it is genuinely traceable to the Indus source, the changed text too may have the same meaning. Thus sabda really means 'bright'. The adjective sagara probably means 'noisy'.

The plurality at the isolating stage was expressed by the

repetition of the syllables three or more times. There are a few such texts. One of them is the following:

rā rā rā ma (fire-pl. death)
= The fires are extinguished.

We do not know which fires are referred to, or whether this is a way of indicating fire in general.

This clause was abbreviated to rāma, which should have originally meant 'ash'. Later, it is said to mean 'a black man', and its patronymic rāmāyaṇi occurs in the AV. Still later, perhaps the comfort provided by the fire gave the meaning 'pleasant' from which the verb ram 'to find pleasure in' developed with its other meanings.

Perhaps there was also another clause with ra, namely ra ma. It was reduced to ram, which seems to occur with the loc. Pl. form raṃ-su (in the ashes) RV. 2,4,5c. Though the pada-text has analysed it as raṃ-su, ram has no place in the Vedic lexicography.*)

Other such texts are obscure.

*)Geldner seems to connect ram (raṃ-su) with the root ram through its doubtful meaning 'joyfulness'. The meaning 'ash' was difficult to be conceived, even if rāma 'a black man' was there.

As a rule, many old monosyllabic words have only luckily survived through their occurrence in the RV. These nág (night), mán (ornament), rám (ash), etc. are only few of them. Similarly, vaṇij, usij, etc. are, perhaps, not derivable from the Vedic roots. Their roots have to be searched in the dust of the Indus language.

The stanza containing this ram (ash), RV 2,4,5 cd may be translated thus: He (the Agni) is recognised with his brilliant lustre in the ashes (raṃ-su) who (even when) grown old has become young again.

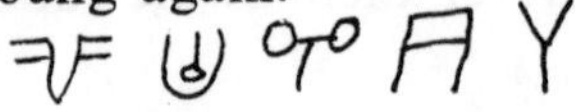

The last sign is definite as to its ṣa-value. Just as yo ṣa (gives pleasure) is supposed to have transited into Vedic as yóṣā (lady, wife), and even a verb yós appears to have developed in yóṣ-i-tvā, we may see the original form of goṣa (RV 9,2,10. 17,2.61,20 goṣa-tama 6,33,5) in goṣa, if  reads like this. It is a bisyllabic verb. A word āguḥ 'an approval call' appears in AB 2,28. and Aśv. śr. 1,5., which may be the fossilised form of ā go ṣa. If ā is the past affix here, it means " past -speak, past-predict, .Then a subject is required which is dha, followed by the object ba. The whole text reads dha ba ā go ṣa and means: the frogs predicted (=has been predicting) the rain.

As compared with and verified from the other texts,  appears to read gau, and even gau ṣa may have evolved as goṣa. Another variety of this sign, that is , is perhaps gāu.

4280 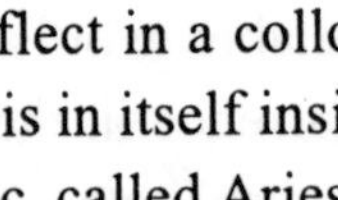

The text appears to be read ba u tū, though the last sign is partially still doubtful as to its real value, The whole text seems to reflect in a colloquial word botū 'he-goat'.Though this animal is in itself insignificant, its name is the first sign of the zodiac, called Aries. As ba is the first syllable of some other words for a 'he-goat', e.g. basta (RV), bakrā (Hindi), etc. ba itself perhaps means a 'he-goat'. It may also be the subject of the clause.

An enigmatic stanza of the RV (1,164,12) comes for reference here, which says: the sleeping ṛbhus then asked;

agohya: who has awakened us? The goat mentioned the dog to be the awakener. At(the beginning of) the year one saw it today.

The Ṛgvedic statement 'the goat mentioned the dog to be the awakener' seems to be the paraphrasing of the Indus clause which says: by the goat the dog is awaened. *)

On the 21st of March every year, the tropical sun enters the sign Aries, which is also the beginning of the star aśvinī. This was originally perhaps the dog star, and śvan 'dog' f. śunī itself was later renamed 'aśvinī'. As soon as the tropical sun comes to the 'dog' star of the 'goat' sign, it is the equinox day, which was then probably the beginning of the new year. Only referring to this, the Indus clause probably informs: the goat and the dog begin the new year.

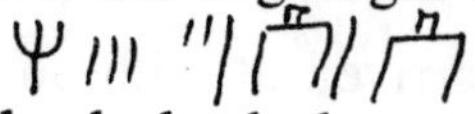

bu la bu la h̲a ta na

bu-la bu-la h̲a ta-na

The reading of this text is nearly definitely correct, though the first and the third sign from the right reads bu only provisionally.

We associate bu with 'water' and la with 'time'. The voiceless h̲ has semantically mixed with the voiced ha in Sanskrit lexicography, and we cannot easily arrive at its meaning, which centres round 'sky' and the ideas associated with it, e.g. 'to say, speak'. Both ta and na, in spite of having several meanings, illude us on their exact idea.

---

*) In the Indian countryside, the domestic dog is called aloud to take its share of food by 'a tū ā' (come dog: hither). This tū is perhaps the 'dog'.

Phonetically, bu la bu la h̲a appear to reflect in the Hindi bulabulā 'the bubbles of water', and the ideas reflected through this word may throw some light on the meanings of the individual syllables.

The transitoriness of the bubbles is wellknown. Therefore, bu for 'water' and la for 'time' appear to say: the waters (in the form of bubbles) last .' The same clause is repeated, probably to emphasise the short duration. It is followed by h̲a (they say). Probably the whole idea (the bubbles of waters last just for a short while, they say) is dependent on the next clause, that is, ta na (womb air) meaning ' in the womb there is air' . The whole text now seems to say: the waters (in the form of bubbles) last for a short time because there is air in its womb.

The meaning which we have arrived at with so much exercise would have been easily conceived by the writer, but we cannot imagine the situation under which this statement was made. This bulabulā was later hyper-sanskritised as budbuda.

The text no. 8002: 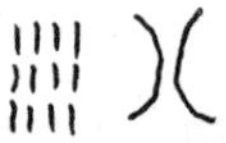

This text should read ī śa, though the ī value for the first sign is only provisional. The word īśa for Siva in Sanskrit occures since R and MBh, though its fem. form īśā meaning 'wealth, possession' occurs in the AV, and its reduced form īś meaning 'ruler, lord' appears in VS 40,1. Its longer form īśāna 'ruler', obviously the present participal form from the root īś 'to rule over', occurs in the RV.

Perhaps the reading of the text is correct, and īśa as a clause may mean: he punishes or inflicts evil. The syllable śa (or the sound ś in general) has originally an evil sense, which is often turned into good only in combination with other syllables.

As a rule, at the isolating stage of the Indus language, an object was referred to by its 'action'. It had no name A river was referred to as 'it flows' Later, it turned into a phrase,and then into a lexeme, either reduced in form due to accent or also with the same body. Thus īśa or īś, initially meaning a 'ruler', became the name of a great chastiser, the lord Šiva.

The Rgvedic version of Śiva is Rudra who, having two r-syllables and probably representing another Indus clause ru da ra (the fire burns the evil), is more ferocious than īśa. In TS he is called krūra, not 'cruel' but 'radiant' like sun, as he is called in the RV. His hot nature gradually cools down till he is the most benevolent of the gods in the classical period. We may like to suggest that Rudra or īśa was the most ruthless police officer, by name or position, one subordinate to the other in rank, of the urban Indus society. In the subsequent pastoral vedic culture he was deified, initially as a god to be afraid of but later a benevolent god.

The vedic mythology is the Indus real history. Agni was the 'enlightener' in charge of education, Indra was the supreme commander in charge of external security, Viṣṇu was a land-survey officer, and so on. These were in the form of clauses at the isolating stage.

8050 **ci h̲a ta ṭha**

The text cited above is remarkable. The first part is the

often quoted phrase, meaning 'truly speaking' The next clause says something remarkable.

The little syllables ta (womb) ṭha (circle) seem to say: the womb turns round, suggesting a meaning 'the father becomes a son and the son becomes a father, and this wheel rolls on'.

When the second syllable was dentalised and deaspirated to ta, the whole clause gradually turned into a phrase and then contracted to a bisyllabic word tata 'father' at the agglutinative stage. That is to say, ta ṭha is the isolating form of the agglutinative tata 'father'. The clause of the agglutinative Indus tata ma-ha (the father has grown old) contracted as tatā-maha on the threshold of the inflexional Indus, meaning grandfather and giving its place to pitā-maha in Vedic it left the scene for ever. Such forms were in vogue long before Pāṇini who quoted these fossilised forms without trying to analyse them. Pāṇini has also quoted a perfect form jā-ha and a pluperfect form ca-ra as suffix, which had already lost their connection with the Indus verbs jā (to be born) and ca (to be) before the Vedic period itself.

The suffix -cara is also tigthly attached with ku in the RV and there is go-cara in Sanskrit, but they are analysed with reference to the verb car (to move).

The Santhal language of today has tata, but it means 'grand father' (both paternal and maternal). It occurs a few times in Vedic, meaning 'father' and corresponds to naṇā 'mother'. In the classical Sanskrit it was replaced by pitā. But later tāta developed from it, which comprises all the near and dear male relations.

There is also nānā meaning 'father 's sister' in Santhal but 'maternal grandfather' and 'elder sister' in Mundari.

In the modern north Indian languages, tāta has variously developed as dādā (elder brother), cācā (uncle) through some *tyatya, etc. with the corresponding fem. forms. Even nānā means 'maternal grandfather' in Hindi and nānī means 'elder sister' in Oriya.

These are the relationship terms of the agglutinative Indus, scattered throughout the country at the grassroot level of the language.

2335 

The whole text is readable phonemically, only the third sign from the right being doubtful, though the text no. 1623 reads the same initial two signs as lu bha. Now the whole text reads: ci ẖa lu bha ta na ma va ṇa ṣa.

The last clause va ṇa ṣa has been interpreted elsewhere: from the waters the life comes. It can also mean: the water gives life to the plants, or, the plants grow through the waters, because the clause has ultimately fossilised as vánas 'plant' (in vánas-páti) and later also as varṣ 'to pour waters', The initial ci ẖa is a phrase meaning 'truly speaking'. The phrase lu bha appears to mean: under the foggy sky.

The clause ta na ma also is almost clear through the clause ta na ṣa (from the womb gems come out). Only the last syllable ma has brought some difference. It may be supposed to mean: in the (womb of the) oyster the pearl matures. This meaning is based on Arthur mee's Children's Encyclopaedia, where the learned zoologist writing on the animal life (Life in the waters, p. 4857 and Fishes of the deep sea, p. 5234) speaks about" nacre, the marvellous fluid, poured out by the oyster when the parasistes escaping from the body of the ray enter the open shells of the shells of the oyster".What the learned zoologist could say in more than one paragraph has been said, though vaguely, by just three syllables in the Indus inscriptions.

Thus the meaning may be finally ascertained as under: Truly speaking, under the foggy sky, the pearl matures in the womb of the oyster (and) the plants grow through the waters.

The fossilised form of ta na ma could be* tarma, for which there is tarman 'the top of the sacrificial post'. However, the meaning of the word of the pastoral Vedic culture does not reflect in the urban culture of the Indus people. When the culture changes, the words of the same stream of the language drastically transfer the meaning. There is a sea change.

From the Indian tradition we know that the pearl comes from the oyster by its taking the rain-water when the sun is in the Svātī constellation (from October 24-5 to November 5-6). Perhaps the phrase lu bha (under the foggy sky) is meaningful only in this respect.

4237 

The text probably reads ra cī ṣa, which seems to reflect in Sanskrit ṛcīṣa 'a frying pan'. As a clause, ra (fire) ca (heat) ṣa (embryo) seems to say: the fire causes heat. Because the heat of the fire is intervened by the cooking appartus, it becomes the point of reference. Therefore, ṛcīṣa means 'a frying pan'.

Even the text no. 2002 reads ra cī ṣa towards the end but, because the central animal sign has been normalised, it is difficult to see cī in it.

Now it appears worthwhile to represent every sign as it

is in the seals . As the animal figures do not admit diacritical marks, the same consonant with different vowels were indicated by slight change in the animal figures.

2151 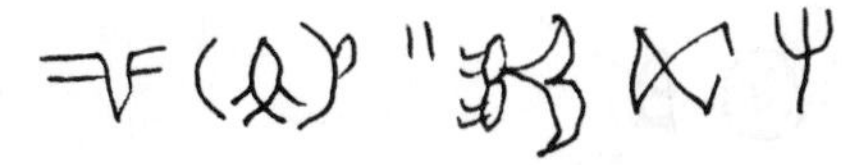

From the pair with h̲a, the third, i.e. the ant-sign for c- from the right appears to be ci (cf. "  = "  ci ha). This ci h̲a, coming in the middle, has semantically contracted to 'and'. It is no more a phrase (truly speaking).

Perhaps ṇa i, contracting as nai and then reduced to nī at some later stage of the language, would have come under the operation of the Pāṇini's rule (6,1,65)" converting the initial ṇ of the Dhatup. to n " That is to say, ṇa ī may be the prehistoric form of the root nī 'to carry, take away'. Then ṇa (life) ī (movement) seems to say: save life.

We have read the bracketed numerals for ṭha and ḍha as ṭho and ḍho, but in case of the present text the bracketing does not indicate o-value for itself. If this bracketed ṇa is read ni, it seems to make a root niṃs with the following ṣa in the Dhātup.

Thus, provisionally, we read the last two signs as niṃ ṣa, occurring a number of times in the Indus texts. Though there are other ways to show ni in the Indus script, the additional anusvāra has necessitated this device here. This niṃs (to touch, kiss) occurs a number of times in the RV.

The syllable ni stands for 'inside' as imaginable from ni-ja 'own', ni-nd' censure' (speak inside), ni-drā 'sleep' (running inside), ni-bha 'like' (reflecting inside), etc,. Therefore, niṃ ṣa may mean: from-inside come-out. It approximates the meanings in the RV. The whole text seems to say: save life and come-out from-inside.

We may compare this statement with the instructions issued by the government and the rescue agencies nowadays in case of earthquakes. The text reads: na ī ci h̲a niṃ ṣa.

4592/5453 

This text appears to be read u ṇu ṣa . If we search for its fossilised form in Vedic, the expected *unus does not exist. But just like * pánus (from pa nu ṣi) further changing into párus (the part of a reed or cane, knot), we may expect that *unus has further changed into *urus, which is used with its extended forms uruṣyati RV, AV, VS uruṣyā RV 6,44, 7 uruṣyu 8,48,5.

The meanings proposed by Roth are based on uru- 'wide', which have been variously manipulated suiting the context. The bane of the Vedic lexicography is that all its vocables are supposed to be connected with some or other Vedic roots. Even Monier-Williams sees the root pṛ in párus, because that is phonetically the nearest. Unless we look to some historical language preceding the Vedic, we cannot reach the original meaning of a word. We have seen elsewhere, manus (a human being) is not one 'who thinks' (from man 'to think') but one 'who is essentially a mortal' (from the Indus clause ma ṇu ṣa).

Because -s- extension in uru-'wide' seems to be unwarranted, we suppose that the word is originally urus - from unus, which may throw some light on the Indus clause u ṇu ṣa on the one hand and on the Vedic passages on the other.

The vowel u is a pronoun (it), being the subject of the clause. In their Vedic occurrences, uruṣyati, uruṣyu are mostly connected with Agni, so that 'light, brightness' may be conceived for ṇu Thus u ṇu ṣa means: It produces light. We know that the meaning of a word jumps like a frog as the latter even slightly changes phonetically. The change of the clause u ṇu ṣa into the lexeme unus and then into * urus is expected, but the meaning has made a long jump in some unknown direction.

Perhaps *unus at the inflexional Indus stage and * urus at the Vedic stage meant 'light or brightness' which was metaphorically used for 'protection, safety', etc. as suggested by Sāyaṇa and Roth, and accepted by Geldner. If * urus is 'light or brightness', the verb uruṣyati may mean ' brightens, helps, renders safety', the action noun uruṣyu is ' helper, protector', whatever the exact meaning in each case.

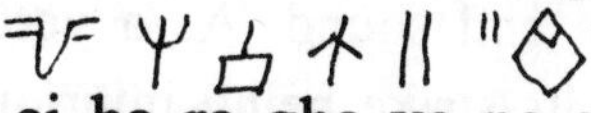

4075 **ci ha ra gha va ṇa ṣa**

There is no doubt about the reading of the text, but the meaning cannot be easily conceived.

The first two syllables, ci ha, make a phrase: truly speaking.

The last three syllables are already familiar to us through the clause of an obscure purport: from the water the life comes (on account of which there is vánas- in vánas-páti 'plant'), in the dwelling there is light, in the body there is charm (on account of which there is vánas 'loveliness' RV 10,172,1).

The remaining syllables in the centre of the text, ra gha, may have fossilised in the following way in the vedic language: it should have been reduced to * ṛgha in ṛghāyate (denom.) and ṛgha-vant (adj.); to ṛc f. (lustre, song) which formed, through its verbal idea arc (to shine, pray), arka (ray of light, sun, fire, song) and arcis (flame). The meanings of these fossilised words and derivatives highlight two ideas, brightness and sound, and these two ideas lurk in the original syllables: ra (fire) gha (sound). Then the meaning of the clause ra gha may be something like this: the fire rattles. As a phrase, it could mean: the rattling fire.

If the last syllable ṣa is connected at the same time with ra gha and va ṇa, turned into phrases, the meaning could be this: the rattling fire produces the cooling brightness.

If we are not accused of flying very high, this may be referring to the " air-conditioned" room of the technically advanced urban Indus society.

The Vedic *ṛgha too should really mean 'lightning' which has both brightness and sound. As a verb, it could have meant 'to thunder', its strike being injurious, as conceived by Sāyaṇa. We see how the noise of the urbanised society linguistically turns into the 'song of praise' in the pastoral Vedic society.

riśādas

The word riśādas is still doubtful as to its real meaning, even though it has been used more than a dozen of times in the RV . It has not also been analysed by the editors of the pada-text, who probably did not know the meanings of the constituent parts.1)

It appears certain that riśa and dasa formed a clause at the agglutinative stage of Indus. At the isolating stage, even ri śa and da ṣa would have been separate clauses. By the time of the Vedic language, the two agglutinative elements, riśa and dasa, did not only contract together but the second element was also reduce due to accent on the second syllable of the first element. It is worthwhile to know the meanings of the individual parts.

The clause ri (speed) śa (evil) at the isolating stage could have meant: let evil go away. As a phrase it could mean: wellbeing, welfare, good luck.

The second part da (sound[2]) ṣa (wise) could have, at the isolating stage, meant:speak wisely 3).

Though with a tremendous long jump, the bisyllabic verb dasa (to speak, say) of the agglutinative Indus seems to reflect in das 'to say' of the modern Punjabi language. The agglutinative Indus clause *riśa dasa should have meant: say wellbeing, wish good luck. When it contracted to riśādas in the Vedic language, it should mean: wishing good luck, sayinjg wellbeing, well-wisher. This is the most appropriate meaning in all the passages of the RV.

In the Indus texts there is a solitary presence of the claus da ṣa  . The first part is not attested.

ẖa ci, ẖa ca

In the following texts, the first three have ẖa ci, and the last has ẖa ca:

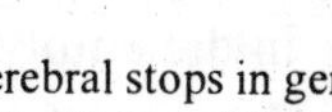 ẖa ci ra

---

1. In a different stanza, kucara has not been analysed. We have found elsewhere, ca-ra is a pluperfact form which should have formed a clause with ku (in oblique case). It was naturally not known to the editors of the pada-text.

2. The cerebral stops in general and the dental voiced stops are connected with" sound". Cf. Lat. Dire. It forms the latter part of vad gad and nad.

3. In a different context, da (mountain) ṣa (be) could also have meant: in the mountains they dwell. It goes well with Dāsa and Dasyu (dwellers of the mountainous villages).

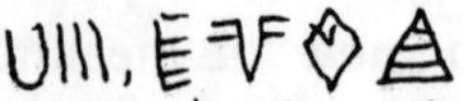 h̲a ci ṣa gha, va ga

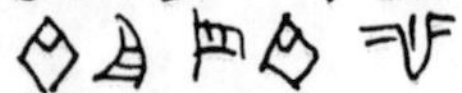 ṣu ci ra h̲a ci

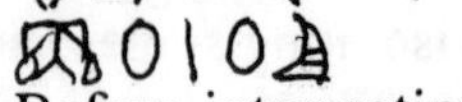 h̲a ca la ca ṭha

Before interpreting the text, we may try to search their cognates in the subsequent stage of the language. While transiting into Sanskrit, h̲a ci should have become śaci (on the analogy of hapta: sapta), which is attested in ŚB 4,1,3,7 and in RV 10,71,6. Either h̲a ci or h̲a ca or both should have been reduced to sac in Vedic on account of the accent on the first syllable, and it is attested as a verb meaning 'to come together' with a number of forms and derivatives.

In Av the final c has behaved as an affricate, and it is represented as haš- in weak forms. In Sanskrit sakhi `companion' the change of h into s has been compensated by the aspiration on the second syllable, and in sāka-m the aspiration has been relieved by lengthening the preceding syllable.

Because the 'empty space' (ha) has association with 'light' (ci), h̲a ci developing the associative sense in sac is natural, and with this meaning let us interpret the Indus texts.

The first text may be identified as'an oblique case + verb + pluperfect': in the empty space,the light, there had been. The second is the future version of the first: in the empty space the light there will be; take care. The third text has two clauses: in the heaven the light there had been; in the empty space the light (there is). In the 4th text, the past affix ṭha at the end stands for two clauses: in the empty space the moon, in the past (time) the moon, there was .

The allusions of these texts may be searched in the later literature. There are several such enigamas in the RV.

1404 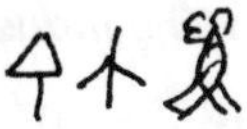

This text seems to be read śa gha ṣa, but in the list of the variants of signs the first sign of this text is remarkably differently drawn. It prompts us to see some other vowel with ś. The fossilised form of this text, which could be either *śaghas or *śakṣa, does not exist. But if we read the text as śi gha ṣa, it may have fossilised as *śikṣa or śikṣā, from which the root śikṣ may have been deduced. This śikṣ is said to have several meanings and has been used copiously in the Vedic literature. But śikṣā is a branch of knowledge dealing specially with the Vedic phonetics. This 'phonetic' aspect of the meaning of the word śikṣā seems to agree with gha of the text meaning 'sound . If we try to interpret this text with this seed-idea, the meaning which emerges is something like this: "śi" causes sound.

Here śi has a meaning something like 'rock, head, cloud', etc. (as one can imagine from the underivable words like śilā, śikhā, śiras, śipi, śiphā, śigru, etc.). A probable meaning may be: the clouds or rocks make noise. How this or similar meaning brought śikṣā to mean ' the science of phonetics' may be the result of some semantic jump.

Whenever we find the remark 'of unknown derivation' in the etymological Sanskrit dictionaries, we are, as it were, exhorted to by-pass the prefix-root-suffix pattern of analysis in the inflexional language. Everything cannot be analysed through the existing material of the Sanskrit language. A good portion of its vocabulary is the inherited property from its mother, the agglutinative Indus (the Sarasvatī).

Many vedic words, bisyllabic or trisyllabic, are still like clauses or phrases of the mother language; e.g. śikhā, śiphā, nabhanu, etc. Some verbal forms of the mother language, e.g. ma-ha (time - perfect)' has grown old', ca-ra (be-pluperfect)' had been, had taken place', etc, ạlready lost their verbal force long before Pāṇini recognised them as secondary suffixes in pitā-maha, etc.Even long before Pāṇini, the ŚB had tried to etymologise śiras (head) by expanding it for * śinas from śi ṇa ṣa as " śirasā bījaṃ harati (Carries seed on head).

We do not imagine any break in the academic tradition form Indus to Sanskrit. Though the society has disintegrated due to some natural calamity, the northern and western branch of the mother language reaching the inflexional stage and the eastern and southern branch limping at the agglutinative stage, there was academic exchange at some level. Therefore, there are agglutinative forms like nabhanu in the Vedic language, unsuccessfully analysed on the inflexional pattern.

1208 

The text most probably reads: ma ṇā ṣa. Its fossilised form *manās was probably further reduced to manā due to the long vowel on the second syllable.

The meanings of manā proposed by Roth (devotion, study, zeal, reflection) have been generally accepted by Monier-Williams, and cautiously utilised by Geldner, because they have been brought near the root man with great strains. Even the denominative manāy is not clear. Evidently, this word is not derived from the Vedic man 'to think', though the original meanings of ma (time) and ṇa (knowledge) of the Indus vocabulary lurk in it.

Referring to the Greek proverbs, namely 'time educates

the wise' and 'time is cure for all inevitable evils' (Teach yourself Greek, pp. 54,55), we can try to reach the heart of this Indus clause; ma (time) ṇa (knowledge) ṣa (embryo) may be supposed to give the following meaning: the time is the source of knowledge or wisdom. Through the meaning 'the knowledge or wisdom acquired through time' at the phrase stage, the clause should have fossilised as manā meaning 'wisdom, inherent knowledge'.

The meaning 'wisdom' at least fits quite well in " cid asi, manā ' si dhīr asi" VS 4,19 (you are cit, manā and dhī). Even the RV 1,173,2. 4,33,2.10,6,3 and 2,33,5 carry the same meaning of manā.

Due to its Indus origin alone, the Vedic anās has been variously interpreted as nose-less (a-nās) or face-less (an-ās), whereas it carries the original meanings of the Indus consonants ṇa (knowledge) and ṣa (vision), that is, a - (deprived of)-nā-(knowledge) s (= ṣa vision). Actually, a-nās means 'ignorant and unwise' said about Dāsas and Dasyus (inhabitants of the mountainous villages), but the meaning has been distorted due to their racial view.

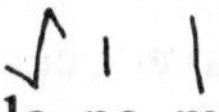

1267 **la pa ma**

This little text had become readable phonetically long ago, but its interpretation has been very difficult. This text, evidently a clause, either subject + object + verb or oblique-case+s+v, did not ever appear to have fossilised as a Vedic vocable.

Theoretically, it should have initially changed as lapama, a phrase, then as *ṛpám, and finally as *urpam. Through this theoretical exercise, it came out that there is actually an ûlapa, said to mean 'bush' (Roth RV 10,142,3 AV 7,66,1).

It is also said to mean 'komalaṃ tṛṇam' (a tender grass). If ulapa has really evolved from the Indus clause la pa ma, we can try to interpret it through the latest meaning.

The first syllable la may have the usual meaning 'time'. As the meaning of the fossilised word ulapa relates to grass, the central syllable pa stands for 'plant'. And the syllable ma may stand for' death' out of its several meanings, because 'time' and 'plant' point to that direction.

The clause perhaps means: in (course of) time the plants die. That is to say, though everything born is destined to die, some plants have a remarkably transitory life. This seems to reflect in a statement of Manu: oṣadhyaḥ phala-pākāntāḥ (the little plants perish when the fruits are ripe). It is thus that they are distinguished form the trees, which endure several seasons.

We appear to have some ground to assume that the Indus clause la pa ma has fossilised as ulapa.

Now we realise how every Vedic vocable cannot be derived from the Vedic materials, roots and suffixes, because a large part of them have been inherited from the mother language. Only rarely are they found in their original forms. As a rule, they have suffered sharp reduction in forms due to accent on the neighbouring syllable.

It is also time to reflect on why such small statements were issued among the public.

1194 

This text can be read with any certainty only at the first syllable. It is śa, and only when the second sign reads pha, we can have an old Vedic vocable śapha (Av. Safa) 'hoof' (of a horse). The third sign probably reads ja, because it represents jatu (a bat) through its pictograph. The whole text may be a clause, comprising subject + object + verb or oblique-case + s + v.

We have generally attached bad meanings to śa, namely 'evil, injury', etc. The words beginning with ś (e.g. śam, śiva, śuci, etc.) gave good meanings only due to the following syllable. The syllable pha is rare in Sanskrit, both initially and medially, and finally it is non-existent. From the available meaning in the tradtional Sanskrit lexicons, we suppose that 'boils, abscess' may be the possible meaning of pha. The syllable ja inherently means 'birth' or the idea associated with it.

The clause means, either:'the injury gives birth ot abscess' or 'from the injury an abscess grows up'.

If the first two syllables suffice to make a phrase, as in many other cases, the verb is ingored, as here. The phrase śapha originally meant 'an abscess through injury'. Later it began to refer to the 'instrument of injury', namely 'hoof'. Because the context of the text is not known, the interpretation cannot be confirmed. Probably it refers to 'hunting', which might be one of the professions of the primitive community. This is the only available text in which all the signs are animal figures, showing that it is one of the earliest inscriptions.

It may be assumed that śap has been deduced from śa pha, and śap originally pointed to a 'physical assault'. Later the meaning shifted to an 'assault by words'. The Vedic śaphā-ruj 'inflicting by śapha' fluctuates between 'assault' and 'curse', as it refers to an 'animal' and 'magician' respectively.

va ta na h̲a ha lī ṣa 

The central sign of the second clause initially appeared to be a combination of la  and ka , but later it began to appear that the combinations like this denote some consonant with a vowel. As a rule, the conjunct consonants are very few in the Indus script. Accordingly, it could be either li or lu (also ki or ku). At least harīṣā 'a preparation from flesh and corn mixed with spices and cooked in butter and water' and halīṣā (said to be = hala + īṣā) of obscure meaning occur in Sanskrit. Accordingly, the clause may be read ha lī ṣa, and the word halīṣā itself seems to distantly reflect in this clause. The meaning of ha (moon) lī (time) ṣa (wise) may be something like this: the moon marks the time, that is, the months are known through the moon (e.g. from full - moon to full-moon, or from star to star).

The first clause, va (dwelling) ta (womb) na (gem) ha (say), appear to mean: in the body (of a woman) the womb shines; it is said. That is to say, the womb is an important part of the woman's body.

The content of the whole text seems to be this: It is said, in the body of a woman, there is prominently a womb. The moon marks the time (of the growth of the foetus in the womb, which is generally 9 solar months and odd days.)

We do not know where this text could have been found, but it is possible that it formed a part of some hospital's inscriptions. The second part of the text is also found separately, also with the numeral sign for ha. It shows that this clause is not dependent on the first, here or elsewhere.

This seems to give some hint about the period of the pregnancy: the moon determines the months. The moon is on the same star at the time of the birth of the child as when it was at the time of conception. For example, if the moon is on the star Kṛttikā at the time of concception, it completes ten rounds when the child is born on the same star. This nearly coincides with 9 solar months and odd days, because the moon makes a round of 27 stars in a little more than 27 days. The stellar month (nākṣatramāsa) consists of 27 solar days.

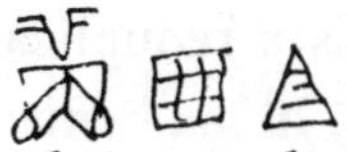

2372 h̲a nu ṣṭha

The text has been rightly read h̲a nu ṣṭha, because it appears to have contracted as anuṣṭhā (RV 1,54,10) of some obscure meaning. Roth conceives this substantive with the adverbial meaning 'soon, immediately', and takes it to be cognate with anuṣṭhu, anuṣṭhayā and anuṣṭhyā, evidently deriving them form anu + sthā.

Though semantically obscure in its Vedic occurrence, its fossilised Hindi form anūṭhā (incomparable, unsurpassable, excellent) may guide us to reach the Vedic and, ultimately, the Indus meaning.

As regards the Indus clause, the final syllable ṣṭha is the verb, the editors of the Sanskrit Dhātupāṭha interpreting sthā as gati-nivṛtti (cessation of movement), clearly identifying the constituent parts (ṣa 'end' = cessation' + ṭha 'disc' = movement) of the root. That is to say, sthā means 'to stay'. Then the preceding syllable nu is the subject, the first ha being the oblique case. The clause symbolically means: in " ha " there is "nu". If nu distantly reflects in na (gem, pearl), it refers to some shining object. Thus the Indus clause may be supposed to mean: in the sky there are bright stars. As a phrase it should mean 'the bright stars of the sky'.

If the Indus clause has contracted as anuṣṭhā in the RV,

the meaning too should have been restricted to 'the bright star'. Then the Vedic verse viśvā anuṣṭhā pravaṇeṣu jighnate should mean 'all the bright stars strike down on the earthly plants'. Perhaps it says: the stars throw their light on the earthly vegetation.

The perfect forms of the root han have given birth to a secondary root ghan, which has a reduplicated weak base jighn- in jighn-ati and jighn-ate. In mathematics, han means 'to multiply ' and har means 'to divide'. Here jighnate refers to the earthly plants multiplying on account of the heavenly light.

Now, the Hindi adjective anūṭhā, the Vedic substantive anuṣṭhā and the Indus clause h̲a nu ṣṭha fall in a line, their phonetic transformation being quite predictable. As we come to the semantic aspect, we notice frog's jump in the meaning from one stage to another : the 'shining object of the sky' has restricted itself to the 'bright star', which has ultimately turned up as 'excellent, the thread connecting the meanings being invisible.

Many Rvedic vocables are difficult to interpret, because they are supposed to have been derived from the Vedic roots. If they are traced back to the earlier stage of the language, the words give the intended meanings of the Vedic poets.

sánutara, sanutár

The vocable sanu- is itself unattested in the RV, but it has at least a derivative, namely sánu-tara adj. (secret, unnoticed). There is also a sanu-tár adv. (away, aside), deviating both in accent and meaning.

We do not imagine a comparative suffix -tara in sanu-tara because its meaning does not support it, nor there is the adverbial suffix - tas in the phonetically impossible sanu-tar. Evidently, sanu- and -tara or -tar are two primitive elements coming together (like pitā-maha 'father + grown old', go-cara and ku-cara of some controversial sense). We have noted elsewhere that the primitive Indus verbal forms have appeared as suffixes, nouns, adjectives, verbs, etc. in Vedic.

The Indus voiceless h is seen sometimes as s (in sapta from h̲a-p-ta, etc,), but sometimes it is silent (in a-śva from h̲a-śva, etc.). A text written in three ways,

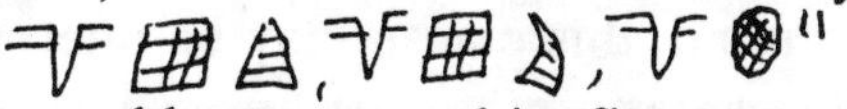

seems to read h̲a nu ṣa, and its first two syllables may have fossilised as sanu- in Vedic. The meaning would be something like this: in the empty space (h̲a) there is continuity (nu ṣa). That is to say, the space is infinite. By the beginning of the Vedic period sanu should have come to mean 'the infinite empty space, the vacuum, the unknown region'.

If ra in -tara is a pluperfect affix. ta (womb) may have the verbal sense 'to cover, contain'. Perhaps ha nu ta ra meant ' the infinite empty space had been covered'. It seems to reflect in the RV 10,129,1c.3. It has fossilised in meaning as 'the covered space, hidden, secret, unnoticed'.

When the adjective sanu-tara was used as adverb, the accent shifted to the penultimate syllable of the last element, causing the final vowel to go (sanu-tár). Its deviating meanings ' away, aside'RV 9,98,11 'far and near 6,51,2 etc. are then imaginable.

The Indus syllable ha does not only indicate the infinity of space but also of time, because both are twin concept. Therefore the Vedic sana (old) presumes a primitive h̲a na meaning 'the continuity of time'. Its extended forms are sanā, sanat, sanatā adv. 'since long', sanaka' old'. The adj.

Sanātana (eternal, permanent) is again a combination of the primitive elements sana from ẖa na with tana, which is the fossilised form of the Indus clause ta ṇa (in the womb it breathes, referring to the foetus in the womb of the mother). Thus, literally, sanātana means 'living for infinity'. Pāṇini conceived it as a suffix t-ana (p.4,3,23) referring to time.

The text  ha nu ṣa may also have fossilised as *anus (which does not exist) and further as arus (cf. P. 4,1,7), which means wound (noun) or wounded (adj.). With this Vedic sense in mind, this clause may be interpreted as follows: the syllable ha means 'horse' among a number of other things, and it is perhaps the voiceless h as in ẖa-śva: aśva, ẖa-r-va: arvā, etc. The central syllable nu may be understood through nud ' to impel' and through luñc for *nuñc (Hindi noc-nā) 'to scratch'. Perhaps nu means 'scratch, wound'.Thus ẖa nu ṣa may be supposed to mean: the horse causes wound.

Gradually, we are discovering 'horse' in the Indus valley even linguistically.

4122 ẖa ta ṇa 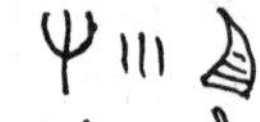
7078 ẖa ṭa ṇa 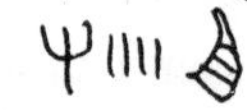

The reading of the two texts is correct as far as possible. If the voiceless ẖ becomes silent and the last syllable is accented at the inflexional stage, the resulting vocable is atná. Fortunately there is atna (sun) according to the Uṇādisūtra, which gives some clue to understand the Indus clause. Thus ẖa (cipher) ta (jewel) na (light) says something like this: in the emptiness a jewel shines. The other text differes only on the second syllable, which perhaps indicates that ta and ṭa differ only phonetically, not phonemically.

It is true, these isolated texts do not give any hint about the context in which they have been said. The clause ultimately contracting to 'sun' semantically suggests that they wanted to make use of the natural light as far as possible, just as now we speak of sun- lamp, sun-cooker, etc.

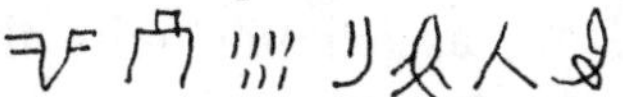

1211 **sa ma na nda ḍha bu ṣa**

This text was read and interpreted in the last work 'The Indus language' p . 81. Then, the first sign from the right was wrongly read as ha, though it was ultimately equated with sa itself in Vedic. As a matter of fact, it is originally sa. Thus the text reads: sa ma na nda ḍha bu ṣa.

There are three small clauses: sa ma, na nda, ḍha bu ṣa. The meanings may be deduced as follows: sa (summer) ma (end) = The summer ends; na (creature) nda (sweet noise) = the creatures are making sweet noise; ḍha (frog) bu (rain) ṣa (embryo) = the frogs bring rain.

The last clause has fossilised as ḍhābus (frogs:at the beginning of the rainy season) in the rustic dialects. The central clause appears in Sanskrit as the verb nand 'to rejoice'. The first clause has contracted as sama (the ending summer) and finally appeared as samā (year), because it was then reckoned from summer to summer.

This is a brief but beautiful description of the nature, when the summer has just ended and it is about to rain. There are two conditions operating simultaneously: on the one hand, the creatures are crying for water and, on the other, the frogs are croaking, predicting the advent of rain immediately.

Though it is difficult to assert that it is the basis of the

Parjanya (RV 5,83. 7,101-2) and Maṇḍūka (RV 7,103) hymns, the situation described there would have been inspired by this little text. At least the RV 7,103,1 opens with the idea contained in the first clause. The second clause seems to reflect in 7,103, 3. The third clause is the basis of the whole Maṇḍūka hymn.

At this stage of our association with the extant Indus inscriptions, we may be in a position to say that these are the textbooks of the Indus society. Because the writing materials like the leaves or barks of trees or similar persishable things were not conceived by those people, they had begun preserving knowledge and information on clay -tablets, animal bones and wood-plates. One can say that Pāṇini was not only aware of the syllabic order of Indus as preserved in the Māheśvarasūtras but also of such whole texts and small clauses as well as of obscure syllables like ghu, ghi, etc. Though they had become meaningless for Sanskrit, he utilised them for his grammar. The meanings of some of them too were known to him; e.g. yū =river, gha = comparison, etc.

The Bird-Signs

Because sa means a 'bird' in the traditional Sanskrit lexicons of the monosyllabic words, the bird-signs of the Indus texts may be indentified as sa. This also seems to be confirmed by a few fossils of the Indus clauses and phrases in the Vedic language.

1338 

This text may be read sa sa ci. The meaning of this text

is not easily conceivable, but the whole clause appears to be fossilised as the Vedic verb saśc (to stop, arrest) with a derivative saścat.

1207 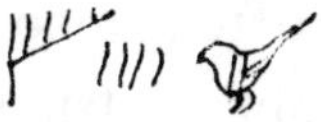

This text, read sa ṭa dha, is attested through the first two syllables saṭa (1. matted hair 2. manes of the horse or lion). It is difficult to say anything more, but saṭa is perhaps a phrase in this clause, being the subject of the verb dha (to shine).

8117 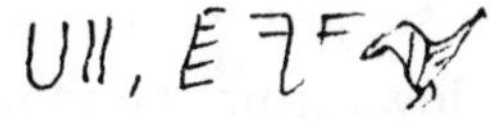

The first part of this text sa ṣa-gha, ra-ga is attested as sasa (grass,corn), though its verbal form sas (to doze,be lazy) is widely apart in meaning. This Vedic fossil of unknown derivation perhaps helps in deciphering the meaning of the Indus text. Perhaps sa itself means 'grass', and the text means: the grass will grow; make haste.

It appears that all the bird-signs represent the specific syllables. Thus in the text 4124 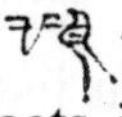 the bird-sign at the right angle is sū. This su ṣa reflects in sūṣ (to give birth to). Even sūṣā and sūṣaṇā appear to be of the same origin.

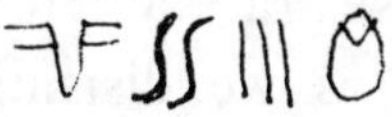

This text,with the field-symbol of a humped bull beneath it, not included by Mahadevan in his compilations, is interesting also graphically. The second sign for va and the third sign for ra are the numerals of the same shape. Therefore, ra has been made wavy to avoid any possible confusion with ha by their coming together. Thus the text reads: ci va ra sa. There is also a smaller text ra sa elsewhere with the field-symbol of a markhor.

Because the Indus c is often also pronounced as an affricate ci may have split as tśi, turning up as śi in Vedic. Then the Vedic version of the Indus text may be: śivarasa, which actually occur s in the RV(10, 9, 2): yo vaḥ śiva (tamo) rasaḥ (whatever auspicious liquid you have).

As we go through the individual syllables in the Indus text, ci (pure)va (water) ra (speed) ṣa (nipple), a clause seems to be formed: adjective + subject + verb oblique case, which means: the pure water flows from the mountain. An urbanised society with a good civic sense is likely to say like this.

By the time of the Vedic language, the phonetically transformed śiva had semantically contracted to "auspicious", and the phrase rasa (flowing from the mountain) too had contracted to just "liquid". As seen through the Vedic transformation, śivarasa (auspicious liquid) marks little deviation from the original, both phonetically and semantically. But in the RV the adjective has been reinforced by a superlative affix -tama, prompted by the exigency of the metre. Briefly, 'the auspicious liquid'.

The independent clause ra ṣa 'flows from the nipple' conveys such ideas as we distantly find in the reduced ṛṣi, ṛṣu and the extended ṛṣa (bhá), though all of them are at the advanced stage of their

---

1) This is contrarily to the general rule, because c generally remains unaltered in Vedic. On the other hand, the Vedic ś corresponds to c in Tamil.

2) The word śiva is otherwise underivable.

3) The verb+oblique case is also to be seen in gāva (goes into the pen).

semantic development: from a ṛṣabhá the animal seed flows; from ṛṣi the thoughts of wisdom flow; and from ṛṣu the light flows.

The humped bull portrayed below the text ci va ra ṣa is probably the precursor of the concept of Śiva riding on a bull in the post-vedic mythology.

In the Vedic period, the phonetically transformed text would have been bifurcated as śiva (auspicious) and ṛṣa, extended as ṛṣa-bha(bull). This auspicious bull was later conceived as śiva-ārūḍha-ṛṣabha (a madhyama-pada-lopi samāsa), and the auspicious god Śiva was made to ride on it.

This is the background of Śiva mounting the bull.The Indus bull may be representing the mountain itself, from which the river carrying fertilising waters flow. At least one field-symbol seems to have indirect connection with the content of the text.

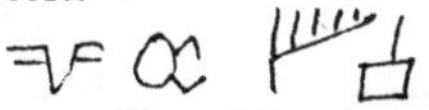

2236 **va dha bha ṣa**

The groups of any two of these syllables reflect in Sanskrit; e.g. va dha in the root vadh 'to kill', va bha in vap 'to sow,' va ṣa in vas 'to live',dha bha in dabh 'to injure', bha ṣa in bhas 'to shine' (cf. bhas-man 'ash'), dha ṣa in dhas (cf. purodhas) and, above all, dha bha ṣa in the devoiced and deaspirated tapas'heat, penance', These syllables may join even in the opposite direction, making dhava reflecting in dhū (cf, dhū-ma 'smoke', dhūp 'sun-light'), bhava reflecting in bhū 'to be', sava reflecting in sū 'to give birth to', ṣa bha reflecting in sap 'come together', ṣa dha reflecting in sadh, and bha dha reflecting in bhad (cf.bhad-ra).

The interpretation of this text may be based on these relexes.Though va has several meanings,'arrow'reflects in vadh ' to kill', 'water'in vap ' to sow', and 'dwelling'in vas 'to live'. The traditional lexicns do not help, but we may associate dha with 'the shining body'. The syllable bha means 'light'and ṣa 'embryo',

In this text, va at the first position is an oblique case followed by the normal clause (s+o+v) dha bha ṣa, which means: the shining body makes light. The whole text means: in the dwelling the shining body makes light. Having the urban Indus culture in mind, we may interpret it thus:in the dwelling the lamp makes light. But this is the simplification of some higher truth. Perhaps the Indus text refers to some physical phenomena:in the universe the sun makes light.

It appears that the oblique case va (dwelling) was a loose element.It was left behind, and dha bha ṣa (the sun makes light) finally emerged as tapas, preserving the most abstract meaning of the concrete fact. The light of the sun is the cause of intelligence (RV3,62,10), which gives spiritual power. Thi s is what is indicated by tapas in its inherent sense.

We may now realize that the seeds of the Vedic language (and of the IE itself) are the individual syllables, not the blanket form of pater, father, vater, etc.

The signboard text of Dholavira

The most noteworthy feature of the signboard text is that it appears to be read from left to right, although usually the Indus texts signs no. 327 and no. 53 are projected in the opposite direction.

As a rule, the projection of the signs is not as significant as its very form, Unless there is any chance of misreading the text, the face of the signs may be projected even otherwise.

Though by the stage of the Brahma script, the left-to-right direction was established, the initial writing at the isolating stage of the Indius language, when words were monosyllabic, was bi-directional. At the agglutinative stage itself, when bisyllabic words and forms had come into being, only one directin had to be chosen, and the choice was in favour of left-to right. In the present text also the directin of writing is from left to right.

Moreover, the 6th sign from the left has ben assumed to be the 124th of the Mahadevan's list, whereas it appears to be the 134th on account of its making pair with 261 and 98. There is no sign-pair of 124 with 261 or 98 in Mahadevan's concordance. Thus the reconstructed text is to be graphically modified on the 6th from the left:

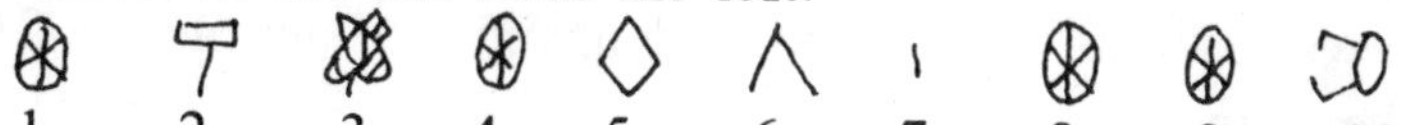

1 2 3 4 5 6 7 8 9 10

The text may be read as follows: ci re pau ci ca ī pa ci ci bha.

On the basis of the reflection of the groups of signs in the later phases of the language, the following clauses may be assumed to be present in this text:

ci re	:	cire 'after a long time' SB, 13,8,1,2.
pau ci	:	poc 'vile' Rām-carit-mānas (mārihi niśicar-poc(that vile demon will kill me).
ca i	:	ce in the Tantric formula vic-ce.
pa ci	:	pac 'to cook' (pacati), paci 'fire' (lex.)

ci bha : cibh, a rustic verb meaning 'to crush under teath to extract juice'. Cf.also cibānā 'to chew'.

When a plant grows and is suddenly cut off at some knot, another stalk or stem develops by its side and the growth of the plant continues. Similarly, when the clause of the isolating stage turned into a phrase, another verb came to lead the agglutinative clause further, at least in imagination. The clause would have changed variously, depending upon the contextual sense, also having the appropriate idea in imaginatin to extend the new clause: ci-re = for a long time (it was calm);pau-ci = (Sudenly) the impending storm (appeared); ca-i = Let it go well; pa-ci = The burning fire (spread in all directions); ci-bha = The lightning -stroke (crushed the people). The words in the parenthesis in the translation was in the mind, seeking appropriate expression through words, appearing differently in different dialects. Finally they resulted as lexical words with semantic jumps in the later phase of the language.

The first clause is physically attested as an obsolete adverb of time. Obviously, ci (time) re (speed)say: the time was passing slowly.

If pau ci reflects in poc,some injurious meaning seems to lurk in the clause. Because ci=to be, pau may refer to 'storm' through pa for 'wind'. Thus pau ci= there was a storm. Through the destruction caused by the storm, the phrase 'destructive storm' might have shifted to something 'destructive', then to 'vile'. A reference to Rām-carit-mānas is not unwarranted. The language underneath Rām-carit-mānas is the agglutinative Indus, the language of the grassroot society, understood far and wide in the country.

If ce in the Tantric formula' cāmuṇḍāyai vicce' is the contracted form of ca i, it should have some good meaning. Perhaps ca i = let there be good (God forbid the evil).

Because pa ci seems to reflect in the verb pac ' to cook', pa may indicate some fiery incident. As a rule, pa stands for 'water' (payas), 'fire' (pāvaka)' wind' (pavana), etc. Thus pa ci=There was conflagration. Even paci =fire in the lexicon.

If ci bha reflects in the rustic verb cibh, bha through its meaning 'light'may refer to 'lightning'. Thus ci bha = there was a strike through lightning.

Perhaps a tragic event is described here:" the time was passing (peacefully). (All of a sudden) there was a terrible storm. Let there be good.(Then) there was a devastating conflagration (and) a crushing blow of lightning". The signboard could have been erected to memorise the tragic event, which later itself fell victim to it.

The isolating stage of a language is not capable of conveying such lengthy messages, but the requirements of the urbanised society had necessitated the use of language beyond its capacity.

1128
ra ṇa gāu 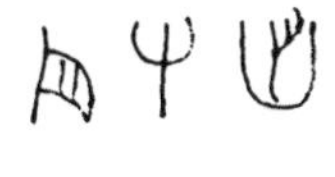

2105
ra ṇa gau 

These two texts have the same sign for ra on the third position from the right. The second sign in each case is for ṇa, but 1128 has the geometrical variety and 2105 the animal variety. Only the first in each case, though apparently a g-syllable, cannot be read any further. Both of them are either the one or the other of the following syllables: ga, gi, gu, gai, gāi, gau, gāu.

Because there is goṇa (ox) in Pali, and Pāṇini also quotes it becoming either goṇā or goṇī in feminine, the two can be read either gau or gāu, because go has already been expressed diacritically  . The two texts read either gau ṇa ra or gāu ṇa ra, meaning the white animal goes (= grazes)/looks beautifull). Because there is gaura 'white' on the one hand and goṇa 'ox' on the other, the two syllables have to be differently read as gau and gāu. Of the two, gāu ṇa may have fossilised as gaura 'white' and gau ṇa as goṇa 'ox'. It is also notable that gāu is far less in number than gau.

Then another text no. 1302 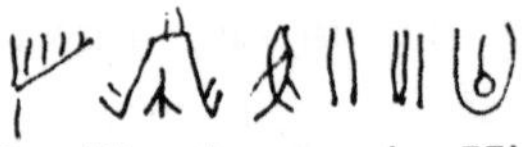 partly reads gau va ra, which has fossilised now in Hindi as gobar 'dung' from *govara. It perhaps decides that  is gau and  is gāu. Thus 1128 reads gāu ṇa ra 'the white animal goes' and 2105 reads gau ṇa ra 'the white animal looks beautiful'. How gau ṇa came to be restricated to goṇa (ox) and gāu ṇa to gaura (white) can be decided by these original meanings.

At the Sanskrit stage, even the Indus clause gā va (goes into the pen) created some confusion, because it became gāu- in the strong forms and gau- in the weak forms.

We are perhaps right in identifying  with gau and  with gāu.

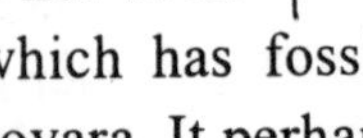

The text probably reads bhū ma na, because the first numeral sign is definitely bha, and the diacritical mark over it is for ū. The next two signs are doubtless ma and na, because this text reflects in the Vedic vocables bhū́man 'earth' and bhūmán 'plenty'.

The meanings of the Vedic vocables can help the interpretation of the Indus clause. The first syllable bhū itself means 'earth', because it has 'brightness' (bha) and 'abundance' (ū).

The relation between sound and meaning has been debated from ancient times. In the modern linguistics, a phoneme is not supposed to have any meaning. It has only the capacity to distinguish meanings. While the mīmāṃsā maintains a permanent relation between sound and meaning (nityaḥ śabdārtha-sambandhaḥ), the Nyāya philosophy says that there is no relation between sound and meaning (śabdārthāv asambandhau). Whatever the later state of affairs in the origin of language, as soon as a sound originated, it had, through its own vibration, some meaning, and it underwent variation as some new elements were added to it. The breathing is originally associated with 'warmth' through its own aspiration: with b, it acquired 'brightness' (bha: bhāti); with d, it acquired 'heat'; with g, it acquired 'burning'.

The next syllable ma stands either for 'water' or for 'happiness', both associated with the earth. The last syllable na (unbroken) may be supposed to stand for 'to continue to exist' through its suggestive meaning. Thus the text bhū ma na means: in the earth there is happiness, or, from the earth the water flows. As a matter of fact, bahu (in plenty) is the loosened form of bhū, which it regains in bhū-yas and bhū-y-iṣṭha.

Even though the Indus society was urban, it was backed by agriculture. Therefore, they emhasised the importance of the earth. The whole bhūmi-sūkta of the AV was based on these tiny clauses. Whatever its inner qualities, the earth is the bestower of happiness.

It appears to be an inscription of the department of agriculture. Now we can form some idea about the whereabouts or location of these inscriptions. Almost all the inscriptions formed parts of the respective departments of the Indus society. Agni and other gods have wrongly been understood as some aspects of nature. They were the real human beings of the prehistoric society.

ba rau ṇa ka ni ka ṣa 

The last part of the text, which also occurs independently elsewhere may be seen in a late Sanskrit vocable nikaṣa 'a touchstone', now derived from ni-kaṣ (the same kaṣ as in kūlaṃ-kaṣa 'eroding the bank', said of the river). This meaning of nikaṣa is the fossilised state of some original meaning: in the stone (ni) the light (ka) sparkles (ṣa). That is to say, the stone is said to sparkle from inside. The verb nikṣ 'to pierce through' also appears to be the abbreviated form of nikaṣa, though the meaning has distanced itself from the original connotation.

The first four syllables ba rau ṇa ka comprise two clauses: ba rau and ṇa ka. The first clause ba (water) rau (fire) appears to say: in the water (there is) fire. This is a primitive way of referring to the lightning-cloud. The thundering of the lightning-cloud, when the clause ba rau phonetically contracted to brū, developed the meaning 'to speak (thunderously)'. Briefly, first of all, the clause 'the water burns' contracted as the phrase 'the burning water' which, referring to the lightning-cloud, was soon transferred to the 'thundering cloud'. This resulted as the verb brū 'to speak'.

The clause ṇa ka (in the knowledge there is happiness) may have turned up as nāka in Vedic, which is explained by the traditional lexicographers as ka 'happiness', a-ka 'absence of happiness' and na-aka 'where there is no absence of happiness'. The element of happiness seems to be the basis of nāka 'heaven'.

The whole text says: in the water, there is fire; in the knowledge, there is happiness; in the stone, the light sparkles.

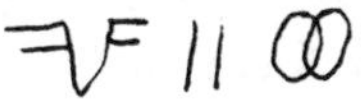

This text may be read cha ra sa. Its shorter version is just cha ra. The initial syllable cha may be both a stop and an affricate. Perhaps the Indus language is peculiar in having voiceless and voiced as well as plain and aspirated affricate, though in articulatory phonetics we know of only plain affricates c and j. When these affricates represent a cluster, they may be split as tś and dź, and their aspirated form may be split as tśh and dźh.

At the beginning of word, the stop element t and the aspiration h may go away. Perhaps the Vedic vocable śara (arrow) represents the shorter clause cha ra, which probably means: the arrow burns, i.e., inflicts burning. The longer clause cha ra ṣa perhaps means: the arrow causes burning.

That is to say, in some cases, the Vedic ś is the result of the splitting of the affricate ch. Similarly, many cases of h in Vedic may be the result of the splitting of the voiced affricate jh e.g. aham from a jha, while it appears to be a stop in the western dialects (Lat. Gk. ego).

When this ś comes to be preceded by a t in the external Sandhi, it becomes an affricate and the aspiration is added over and above. This ch is naturally not an integral sound but a cluster. In the language of the RV, even an original ch is an affricate, a consonant- cluster, so that there is "ga-cha-ti" for the usual "gacchati". It seems that by the time of

Pāṇini ch had become an integral sound which required the insertion of c.

This is probably a single case in the Indus texts through which the sign for cha seem to be confirmed.

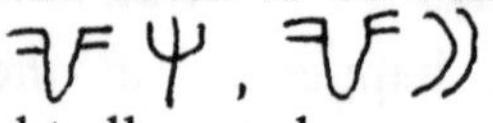

The texts undoubtedly read ṇa ṣa, which may have been a clause. Its fossilised form in Vedic could be nas (nose). Since the meaning of the fossil is confirmed, the clause na (life, breath) ṣa (end) seems to say: the breath stops (= the life comes to an end). The organ through which it could be ascertained that the life has come to an end was naturally designated as nas (nose). In compounds it is also in its full form: un-nasa (high-nosed).

Another text 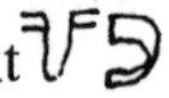 ṇā ṣa appears to be fossilised as nās, but its meaning is controversial. The editors of the pada-text and Sāyaṇa, who were unaware of the term 'ethnology', analysed it as an-ās (faceless), but the British ethnologists analysed it as ā-nās (noseless) and applied this term to the Dravidians.

The syllable ṇa stands for 'knowledge' and a-nās really means 'without knowledge, ignorant, unwise', which was the appellation of the Dāsa and Dasyu groups who dwelt in the mountainous villages (da = mountain, sa = fence). Accordingly, the clause ṇā ṣa may be supposed to mean: the knowledge is acquired, which is a custom of the city-dwellers.

The limited vocabulary of the primitive people was generally extended by context in which it was used. Therefore, we are perhaps justified in drawing any meaning from the context. Of course, the texts of the Indus inscriptions have hardly any definite context.

(A-a)

Before the isolating Indus transited into the agglutinative stage with some grammatical elements, it introduced some ideas by the bending of the vowel a of the verb ṣa of the first clause towards u. By this bending, the two clauses appeared to be related.

Only a few definite or less doubtful texts may be taken into account.

4147 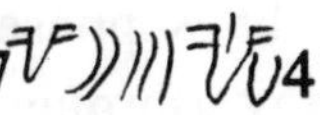 4132 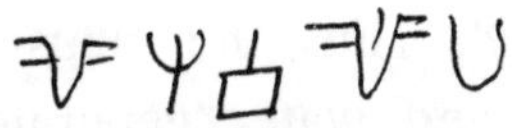

ga ṣu va ṇa ṣa (plant grow water life give)
=Plants grow (when) water gives life.

The two clauses seem to be related through the conjunction "when", expressed by the u-bending of the verb ṣa.

At the inflexional stage, the first clause ga ṣu is seen reduced to gaccha (tree) through Prakritism. We will see later how a compound *gaccha-vṛkṣa emerged, which we may find in the colloquial gāchh-brichh (trees and plants).

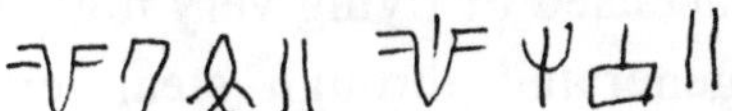

1081 **ra va ṇa ṣu, ra na bha ṣa**

The reading of the text is doubtless. The va ṇa ṣu group of the first part and the na bha ṣa group of the second have fossilised as vánas (in vánas-páti 'plant') and nábhas, which have of course helped in the interpretation of the original clauses.

In this text, the initial ra in each case has disturbed the earlier grouping. The verb of the first clause bending towards u shows the syntactical relation of this clause with the following. The last syllables ṣu and ṣa being verbs, the preceding ṇa and bha in each case should be the object. The initial ra va and ra na of the two clauses should be phrases as subject. The structure of the two clauses may be stated thus:

rava (s) ṇa (o) ṣu (v), rana (s) bha (o) ṣa (v).

Some fossilised form of rava is not to be seen. Therefore, the two syllables have their original sense: fire (and) water. Suiting the context, ṇa may be taken to mean 'energy'. Thus the clause may be supposed to mean: the fire and water generate energy (through the steam).

The syllabic group rana of the second clause appears as ráṇa 'joy' in Vedic. If ra (speed) and na (body) was itself a clause at the earlier stage, it could be 'energy'. The whole clause probably means: the energy generates light.

Now the whole text seems to say: If the fire and water generate energy, the energy generates light. The energy of the urban culture turned into joy of the pastoral culture.

If we are not accused of flying very high, this may refer to the energy generated through steam-engine and the electricity generated through it. Here, in the urban Indus society, we come across machine converting mechanical into eletrical energy. Can we believe it?

2300 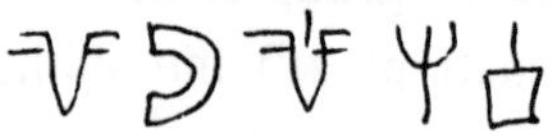

va ṇa ṣu ṇā ṣa (water life give known be)
=The water gives life (as) it is known.

Here the u-bending has connected the two clauses in a

different way. The second clause ṇā ṣa was reduced to nās at the inflexional stage, probably meaning 'knowledge', and in the RV it has made a compound with the privative a-, a-nās meaning 'devoid of knowledge, ignorant'.*

4131 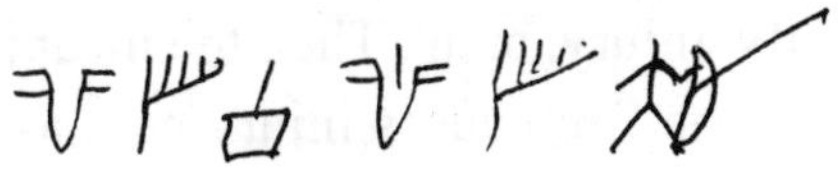

rau dha ṣu va dha ṣa (sun bright be water wealth be) = (If) the sun is hot, the rain is in plenty.

The meaning is based on common sense, though rau for 'sun' and va for 'rain' are doubtless. The first dha (light) for 'hot' and the second dha for 'plenty' are again based on common sense. The verb ṣa bent towards ṣu in the first clause suggests "if" connection.

The first clause may have contracted as ródhas, Av. raodah (stream), and the deaspirated rodas in rodasī (heaven and earth) may be even semantically related with it.

The first two syllables, rau dha, may reflect in the colloquial Hindi raudā (the heat of the sun). But va dha ṣa does not semantically reflect in the phonetically contracted vádhas (weapon). Perhaps the 'plenty of rain' would have become deadly through floods. Thus weapon may be the secondary meaning of vadhas.

This text may be understood even otherwise. If rau is

---

*In the Vedic lexicography, it has been confused with nas 'nose' and said to mean 'noseless', giving a racial interpretation of the word.

This meaning has been attached to Dāsa and Dasyu, which too have been understood racially as 'non-Aryan'. As a matter of fact, they were simply "villagers", the inhabitants of the countryside (the modern dehāt, dih or deh reflecting in dasyu), the outlawed groups of the same Vedic communities.

taken in the ordinary sense of 'fire' and the meaning 'arrow' for va is taken into account, dha, being the first syllable of dhanus (bow), of dabh (to injure) from the original *dhabha, of dhamati (blows), of dah (to burn) from the original *dhabha, may signify 'injury, pain'. Then the meaning of the two clauses may be: the fire causes injury/pain as much as the arrow causes injury/pain. In this way, vádhas meaning 'weapon' can be explained.

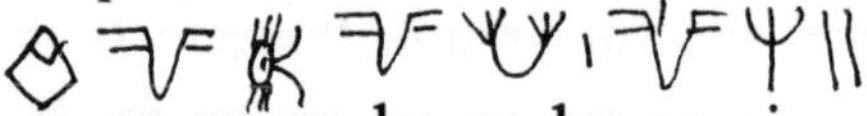

2687 ra ṇa ṣu pa ka ṣa bu ṣa ci

This, a little long text, is hardly coherent in meaning. But it is the earliest example of a stanza in Gāyatrī metre. Just as a typical Gāyatrī stanza contains nine ideas, often coinciding with nine words, this Gāyatrī stanza of the isolating stage, contains nine syllables. In the Vedic stanzas some particles come to make 8 syllables in a verse, because the Vedic words are not uniform in size, but they hardly contain more than 9 ideas even in young hymns.

Of the three clauses, the first should have contracted as *raṇas, which is unattested. The second clause may be seen in the contracted pakṣa 'wing'. The third clause is in the passive voice, the object preceded by the verb, a typical trick at the isolating stage, having no morphology.

But it is remarkable that ra = fire, pa = air and bu = water appear as subject, the object being knowledge (ṇa), joy (ka) and light (ci) respectively, the verb remaining the same. The 'heat' being a source of intelligence is known to us, the cool air is enjoyable, but the water being the source of light transgresses our scientific knowledge. Does it refer to hydro-electricity?

2263

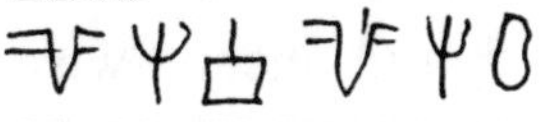

ca ṇa ṣu va ṇa ṣa :

1092

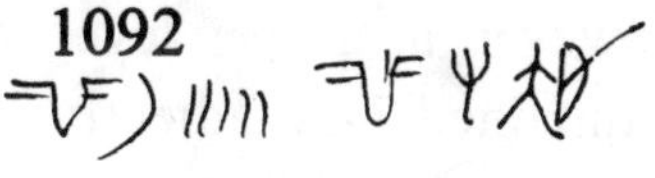

rau ṇa ṣu ca na ṣa

The two texts are structurally similar. Phonetically they are easily recognisable, but semantically they are vague.

Because there is ca ṇa ṣu, there may also be ca ṇa ṣa, and both ca ṇa ṣa and ca na ṣa have converged as cánas in Vedic. The Vedic cano-dadhīta is said to mean 'may accept, may find pleasure in'. Then perhaps cánas is 'agreeableness'. That is to say, the distinction between the original ca ṇa ṣa and ca na ṣa has been lost in the Vedic cánas. It appears that the syllables ṇa and na do not say anything specifically different.

But the further reduced form of cánas is carṣ, and its solitary derivative carṣ-aṇ-i makes the difference: with one meaning it is an adjective, with another meaning it is a noun. These two meanings may derive from the two different clauses at the isolating stage:

ca ṇa ṣa: ca na ṣa

Perhaps ṇa refers to abstract qualities (knowledge, etc.) but na to concrete objects (gem, etc.). They may have led the meanings slightly apart:

ca ṇa ṣa = The moon causes intelligence.

ca na ṣa = The moon causes gem=brilliance.

Now the two texts above may be brought here.

ca ṇa ṣu va ṇa ṣa = If the moon causes intelligence, the water causes life.

rau ṇa ṣu ca na ṣa = If the sun causes intelligence, the moon causes beauty.

If the meanings were confusing in the original, it is not surprising if they converged as a single cánas in Vedic.

However, at deeper level, the distinction in meaning was maintained. As adjective, carṣaṇi should mean 'wise, intelligent' and as noun it refers to 'people', possessing beauty,wealth.

The Indus drainage system

The following two texts are identical on the first three signs, which form a clause, its verb bent towards u, which shows that the following clause in each case is semantically related with it.

2355 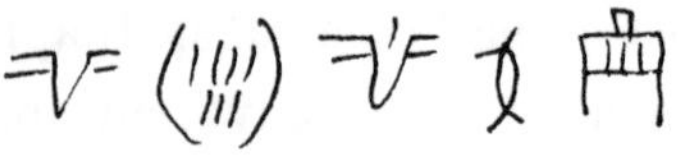

6227 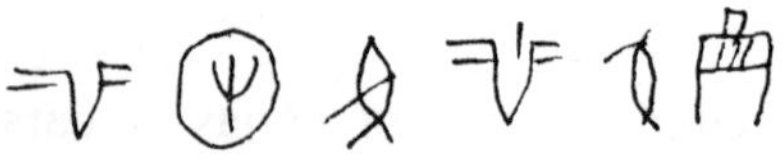

The difficulty lies in the first two signs which are doubtful as to their phonemic values. The basic graphic structure of the first sign is , which we like to identify with ba. But this ba itself is not available. The additions to this basic structure are more than one in the following sign, which appear to be the typical vowel-markers

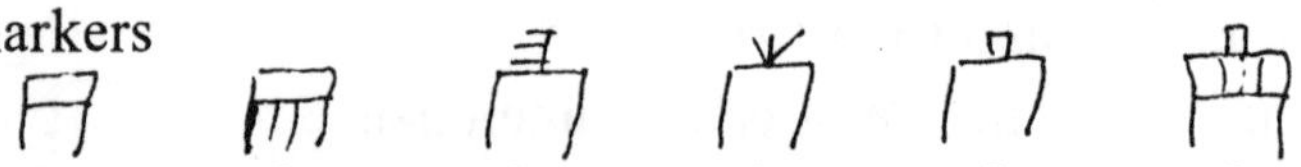

1 2 3 4 5 6

The 1 could be identified with bā, 2 with bī, 5 with bu and 6 with bū, others being unidentifiable even provisionally. The 6th being bū is also provisional. The second sign is a composite one, probably j-ña. The possibility of jña being a ligature in Indus cannot be ruled out, because k-ṣa, t-ra and j-ña are typical ligatures in all the Indian scripts down to the present day. In Indus there are also k-ṣa 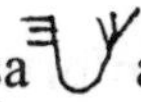 and t-ra  .

There is some difficulty in ascertaining the meaning. Perhaps bū (drainage or sewer water, cf. mod. Persion bū 'smell') j-ña (poisonous and contaminated) ṣu (be) say: if the sewer water is poisonous and contaminated.

The next clause of the first text perhaps reads: ḍho ṣa. It is identifiable with the colloquial ḍhos (a local instrument for siphoning waters). ḍho ṣa means: through an instrument we siphon out the water.

The whole text says: If the sewer water is poisonous, it is siphoned out. The instrument called ḍhos is even now used in the country side for siphoning waters.

The second clause of the second text reads ma ṇu ṣa. It has fossilised as manus in Vedic. Because we try to derive all Vedic words from the Vedic roots, the original meaning is bound to be misled. A man is mortal; therefore ma (death) ṇu (certain) ṣa (be) has fossilised as manus (one destined to die) meaning 'a man': If the sewer water is poisonous death is certain (to its user).

The clause ma ṇu ṣa also occurs elsewhere:

2534 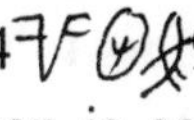 9001 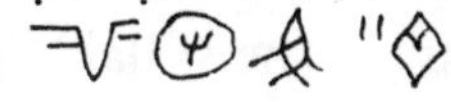

A man is certainly a mortal, and this idea reflects in manus which goes to the Indus clause ma ṇu ṣa.

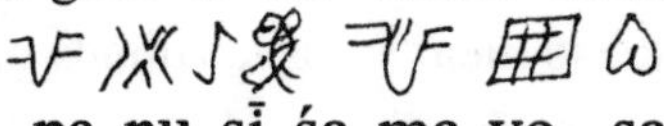

3094 **pa nu ṣi śa ma yo ṣa**

The reading of the text is correct as far as possible. The last four syllables are already familiar to us as to their meanings: the evil ends (and) the camfort is there, or, let the evil end (and) the comfort be there. They have fossilised as śám (well-being) and yós (welfare, comfort)in the language of the RV, the former continuing even later, but the latter only as a suffix (cf. P. 3,2,170).

The first three syllables are new, but the verb bent towards i indicates some syntactic relation between the two parts of the text. The normal clause should be: pa nu ṣa. Its fossilised form in the Vedic language may be *pánus, for which there is panu- in the RV 1,65,4. Its meaning here is obscure, but it appears to reflect in párus, a further fossilised form of *pánus, in VS 13,20: growing forth from stem to stem, going from one knot over to another, o sacrificial grass, thus make us expand in thousand and hundred.

That is to say, panu is not quite different from párus, and concretely it means 'stalk' or 'distance from one knot of a plant to another'. Speaking botanically, a plant grows knot by knot, stem by stem. As the tip of a plant grows further, a knot is formed at the last stem. Abstractly, panu with its instrumental form means 'gradually': the waters make it grow gradually (RV 1,65, 4c).

Now we have some ground to peep into the meaning of the Indus clause pa nu ṣi. The syllable pa refers to a 'plant', which is the first sound of this word itself according to linguistic embryology. The next syllable nu stands for 'continuity'. The clause means: just as plants grow continuouly (from one knot to another)......

Now the next part of the text may be brought:........, the evil ends and comfort comes. The whole text may be translated thus: Just as plant grows on (from one knot to another), the evil ends and comfort comes (gradually).

We see how the pastoral Vedic culture has modified the

refer‿end of the urban Indus culture, from botany to ethics and metaphysics.

The Vedic ṛbīsa

A strange word ṛbīsa, meaning 'an abyss, chasm ' (in the earth from which hot vapours arise) occurs at least four times in the RV (1,16,8. 117, 3. 5, 78, 4. 10, 39, 9), every time involved in some kind of trouble for Atri, who was rescued by the Aśvins. Elsewhere the meaning is somewhat updated, its being a cavity in the earth where fruits are matured. Thus ṛbīsa-pakva means 'matured in abyss', not fit for eating. In the countryside, a cavity is dug in the earth to mature specific fruits by warming them through the moist heat of the fire.

Just as ṛtá (the regular order of the universe) goes through *rata to the Indus la ṭha (the time rolls on), we may postulate an earlier ra bī ṣa for the Vedic ṛbīsa.

As a matter of fact, 'an abyss in the earth from which hot vapours arise' requires the involvement of fire and water, for which the syllables ra (fire) and ba (water) should have been employed. In the following text, the first three signs appear to be read ra bī ṣu:

4304 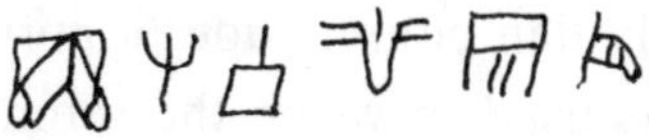

The verb bending towards u shows the syntactical relation of this clause with the following. It appears to say: When the fire heats the water ....

The following clause va ṇa ṭha of the same text should have fossilised in Vedic as *vánat. But because the accent has shifted to the second syllable, the final t has been voiced in vanád meaning 'fire', on account of which Grasmann has analysed it as van-ad (wood-consumer).

The stanza (RV 2,4, 5 ab) containing vanád. may be translated thus: What they (the priests) extol the immense power of mine, the fire, that (extoling) makes, as it were, the praise for the priests.

Though *vanat itself is unattested, its further reduced form vant = vart (vṛt) 'to turn round, roll' is there. In this case, perhaps, the clause va (dwelling) ṇa (breath) ṭha (disc) seem to mean: (When the fire heats the water) in the room the vapour circulates.

Even another meaning is possible for the whole text: when the fire heats the water, in the machine the wheel rolls. We appear to fly very high, but let us put up with it.

In a different context, va ṇa ṭha may also mean: in the dwelling the fire turns round, that is, the fire is carried from house to house. Just fifty years ago in the countryside a girl had to run from house to house in search of the fire.

The same text may also say: the wind (va) wrecks (ṭha) the ship (ṇa), the first clause slightly changing its meaning: when the heat evaporates the water. Here also we appear to fly very high, but let us remember that the Indus society was technically advanced.

Even now in the Indian countryside, a portable earthen cavity carrying fire is used to warm the room. It is called borsī. It may be the corrupt form of ṛbīsa. It is a primitive form of the central heating.

The ṛbīsa would have been a centrally heated room where the Atris of the fire-brigade, feeling suffocated and facing danger of life, would have been rescued by the Aśvins of the rapid action force. It is true that the RV often sings the glorious history of the urban Indus culture. There was no break in the tradition of the Indian people in passing from the urban to the pastoral culture.

In the seal bearing the inscription ra bī ṣu va ṇa ṭha, there is "a man armed with a sickle-shaped weapon facing a seated woman with dishevelled hair and upraised arms" (Mahadevan).

The first clause ra bī ṣu fossilised as ṛbīsa in Vedic and second clause va ṇa ṭha fossilised as vart (vṛt)/vanád are at the two ends of a stupendously long dark period. Neither the primitive nor the fossilised state of the inscription shed any light on the events which took place in the dark period, but the socalled field-symbol of the inscription and the horrifying experiences of the Atris described in the RV (1, 116, 8. 1, 117, 3. 5,78, 4. 10, 39, 9) appear to say something.

The woman with the dishevelled hair and upraised arms just portray the possible suffocation in the centrally heated room or any difficulty with primitive type of machinery, and the man nearby with sickle may portray the member of the rescue operation. Perhaps there is an instruction to raise alarm in case of emergency, so that immediate help could be made available.

Even now, near a high voltage electric station we find the skeleton of a skull between two arms with the inscription: danger. That primitive urban culture also sent similar messages to its people. We have used just one word (danger), but they used two clauses (with "if - then").

With the same text there is another field-symbol: Nude female figure upside down with thighs drawn apart and a crab (?) issuing from her womb; two tigers standing face to face rearing on their hindlegs at L. (Mahadevan).

On each seal with the same text,there are two

field-symabols, one at the right side and the other at the left side, probably because there are two clauses joined together through the conjunctions if - then. Just as the clauses are conjoined, the two field-symbols in each are related:

1. raising alarm: rescue operation
2. escape from danger: medical treatment

Now it appears certain that as and when texts become legible syllabically and comprehensible in meaning, the field-symbols will be properly understood as to their exact symbolism.

The text ra bī ṣu va ṇa ṭha has perhaps given a coherent meaning: if the fire heats the water, the vapour (dangerously) envelops the room. But three other texts with the same va ṇa ṭha as the second clause in the same line are hard to be digested.

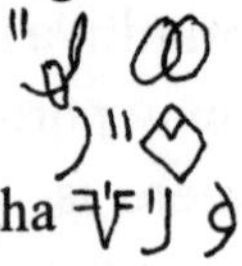

cha sa ha

ci ha na

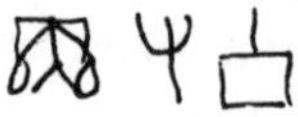 va ṇa ṭha ni nda ṣu

The first clause is completely dark, having no reflection in the later phase of the language, though phonetically it is not quite uncertain. The seccond clause perhaps reflects in the late Sanskrit vocable cihna 'mark, sign, indication'. The third clause also appears to reflect in the Sanskrit verb nind 'to abuse, censure'. Perhaps va ṇa ṭha has either the same meaning in all the texts or the meaning differs according to the prece-ding clause. It has fossilised either as vanád (fire) or as vart (to roll), which should reflect in their clause form.

The dark clause may be totally ignored for the present.

Then ci ha na - va ṇa ṭha seems to have fossilised as cihna (mark) - vanád (fire)/vart (to roll). It hardly says anything more than: the mark (caused by) the fire, or, the mark recurs. The distance between the two phases of the language is so great that the two fossilised vocables do not indicate their relationship at the clause stage. An ancient proverb 'the gold is tested in the fire' perhaps helps in interpreting ci h̲a na: the gem is heated in the fire. Perhaps distantly we can imagine: just as a gem is heated in the fire, the foetus matures in the human body.

The third text, fossilised as nind - vart, also does not take us to its meaning at the clause stage: ni nda ṣu (if there is sweet sound inside) va ṇa ṭha (the life vibrates in the body). The meanings of the two clauses are not coherent. But if we recall an ancient tradition of the countryside in which 'the poisoning effect of some plant in respect of an animal is removed by chanting sweet sound in its ear', we can render the text thus: if the sweet sound is produced in the ear, the animal comes to life.

This is how we can say that the messages of the Indus inscriptions are embedded not only in the Vedas but also in the folklore of the Indian countryside. There have been just a few seers who could know this truth, some by intution and some by oral tradition.

A slightly changed order of the second clause, that is 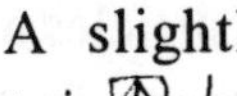 ṇa va ṭha gives an altogether different meaning.

The word nod, unaccented, AV 5, 19, 1 and SB 2, 4, 3, 2 has been analysed in the pada-text as na+ut, which simply suggests that ut is some obscure vocable. This ut can be searched in the ruins of the Indus language. Like sát traceable to ṣa ṭha, ut may be traced in some *uṭha. The Indus text ṇa va ṭha quoted above may be brought here. The phonetic transformation of va ṭha into ut/d cannot be ruled out, and ṇa va ṭha may have ultimately fossilised as not/d through navat/ |navad, but how it lost its genuine accent has to be examined.

If va (water) ṭha (disc) mean something like 'the water is poured', ṇa appears to be an oblique case and probably means 'earth' on which the water is poured from the sky. That is to say, ṇa va ṭha means: On the earth the water is poured.

While being contracted to *nód/t phonetically, it became an adverb with local sense meaning 'from the earth' and, therefore, lost the accent.

Thus

atimātram avardhanta nod iva divam asp̣ṛśan = They grew extensively; from the earth, as it were, touched the heaven.

not parābabhūvuḥ = disappeared from the earth.

Roth takes this adverb to mean 'almost.'

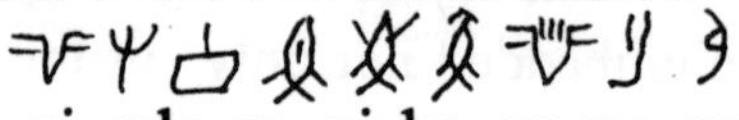

4104 ni nda ṣo ni ha nu va ṇa ṣa

Just as a typical Rvedic stanza in the Gāyatrī metre expresses nine ideas in exactly nine words, the particles and expletives excluded, this is a typical Indus stanza in the primitive Gāyatrī metre.

Of this stanza, the last verse is already familiar to us through other texts. If, in a different context here, it differs in meaning, that is not a point to be debated. The clause va ṇa ṣa has fossilised in Vedic as vánas 'plant' (in vánas-páti), later also as varṣ 'to rain', though it is also said to mean 'beauty' and 'desire'. The root van itself, deduced from vánas, is said to have a number of meanings, perhaps concealed in the different meanings of vánas: to love, desire, gain, win, prepare, hurt, sound, serve, honour, worship, etc. All these meanings are not attested, because the word itself was about to disappear when it was somehow arrested by the Vedic hymns.

Two meanings may be proposed for va ṇa ṣa namely:

From the water there is life.

In the dwelling there is light.

As it is the last clause of the text, its meaning should be congruent with the preceding two clauses.

The first clause reads: ni nda so. Its first two syllables have fossilised as the verb nind 'to censure, condemn', the whole clause fossilising as *nindas, which is unquotable.

The second clause reads: ni ha nu. Its last two syllables have fossilised as hnu 'to hide from', ni-hnu also meaning 'to deny'.

The fossilised forms of the three clauses of the whole text, *nindas nihnu vánas, meaning 'censure denial love, respectively go widely apart and a congruent and coherent meaning is naturally out of question. Even if we attempt interpretation from the Indus point of view, we have to depend on the Sanskrit vocabulary:

ni (inside) nda (sweet sound) ṣo (embryo) appear to say: let there be sweet noise indside = one should speak sweetly, or, if one speaks sweetly. In the fossilised verb nind, the sweet sound has perverted into 'censure'.

ni (inside) ha (voice, word) nu (to hide) appear to say: let one hide words inside = Untrue words should not be spoken, or, one should speak truly.

Perhaps the first clause was paraphrased in Sanskrit as priyaṃ brūyāt, and the second as 'satyaṃ brūyāt'. Now the whole text should be understood coherently as follows: if one speaks sweetly, if one speaks truly, there is wellbing in the house.

When the Indus clauses were fossilised phonetically, the crippled Vedic vocables could walk only through sticks in the form of "fillers", the ideas which were only in imagination: *nindas = sweet words (before it degenerated into 'censure') had a filler like 'when they are spoken'; nihnu = true words (transferred from 'hiddenness') had a similar filler; and vánas = love, beauty had a filler like 'there is' (also unexpressed).

When ra bī ṣu va ṇa ṭha were fossilised as ṛbīsa (a cavity in the earth, but originally 'a centrally heated room') vanád (fire) before the beginning of the Vedic language, these crippled vocables needed some stick for walking. Before they parted asunder in Vedic connected with different episodes, they would have walked together with some fillers: ṛbīsa = the centrally heated room (became suffocating, because) vanád = fire (heated the water to raise vapour).

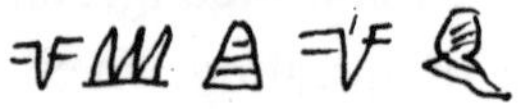

1289 la ṣu ẖa da ṣa

The first clause la ṣu, syntactically connected with the following as indicated by the u-bending of the verb, appears to reflect in the Vedic ṛṣu (through rasu) of doubtful meaning. The syllable la changing into ra may suggest 'fire', thence 'flame' (Roth), but the original meaning of la is 'time', thence 'movement', as suggested by Sāyaṇa.

As a clause, la (time) ṣu (embryo) appear to mean: when the time came into being, as the time arose.

The next clause h̲a da ṣa reflects in the Vedic sadas (seat, abode). But because da also stands for 'sound' (in va-d, na-d, ga-d) sadas may be a 'resounding abode'. Thus h̲a da ṣa means: in the emptiness a resounding abode emerged.

The whole text seems to say: Just as the time arose, the resounding space emerged in the emptiness.

This seems to suggest that 'the time and space arose simultaneously'.

5986 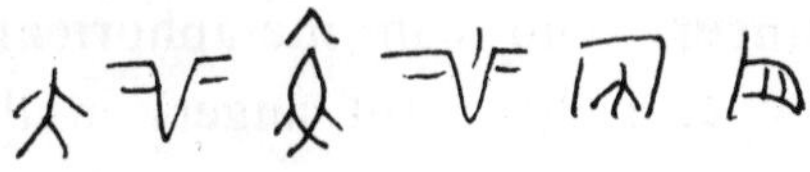

The second sign of this text is obscure even graphically. We have seen that the b-syllables are graphically integral. Therefore, it is an altogether different syllable. If the Vedic vocable ṛjīṣa reflects in the first three signs, we may read it ra jī ṣu (fire/speed energy embryo) which may give the following meaning: from the fire energy may come. The second clause, in passive voice, may mean: in the interior speed is caused. Thus the whole text means: Because the energy comes from the fire, speed is caused inside. This is a statement of the urban Indus society, advanced in the technical knowledge.

Though the Vedic fossils, ṛjīṣa and nisara, are still obscure to their real meanings, we may try to interpret them through the Indus clauses.

Because ṛjīṣa qualifies Indra, it may have the meaning 'fiery or energetic' in the RV (1,32,6). In its later occurrences, it is said to mean 'husk', but still it has some relation with the fire. Still later it is said to mean a 'cooking vessel' frying pan', which too shows its relation with fire. Thus ṛjīṣa is the burning power of the fire, reflecting other ideas like 'energy, speed'.

Taking the meaning of the Indus clause into account, we think that nisara as a lexical word would have referred to some professional (similar to an iron-smith) in the urban Indus society. In VS 30, 14 there is a peculiar equation:

manyu (anger): ayas-tāpá (iron-smith)

krodha (anger): nisara (?)

Here, nisará must refer to a mechanic, which could be a steam-engineer, who can metaphorically stand for a 'controller' i.e. pacifier (of anger) in the Vedic. In the transition of the urban into a pastoral culture, there was a drastic change in the referends of the primitive words.

Thus 'a centrally heated room' could become ṛbīsa 'an abyss', 'the decocted chemical liquid' could become yūs 'soup, broth', 'the flowing water' could become rasa 'juice', and so on. It is not surprising if the 'steam-engineer' of the urban Indus society should have become 'a pacifier'.

(B)

The Agglutinative Indus

Now we come to the next stage of the language which was agglutinative. The following texts are actually quotable:

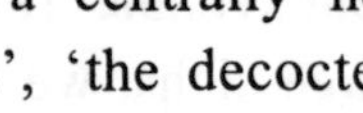

4378 **dra-gha, ra-ga (conflagration-future, speed-order)**
= There will be a conflagration; do run away.

Perhaps drāg (immediately) is the fossilised form of the clause.

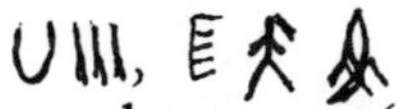

4588 pra-gha, va-ga (storm-future, arm-order)
= There will be a continuous storm; do take care.

The adverb prāg (from the east, formerly) appear to be the fossilised form of this clause. Perhaps the eastern direction was stormy.

4479 ha ṭha, ra-ga (sky-circle, speed-order)
= The sky rolls (hither); do run away.

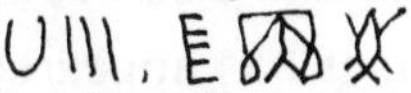

4489 ha ṭha-gha, va-ga (sky circle-future, arm-order
= The sky will roll (hither); take care.

Perhaps the 'sky' refers to avalanche, which used to sweep away the primitive men and animals in the glacier ages (Arthur Mee: The Children's Encyclopedia p. 168).

These texts take us thousands of years back when the forefathers of these writers used to advise their fellowmen about the impending catastrophe and the necessary precautions. Perhaps these text-writers themselves were prone to similar catastrophes.

Really speaking, these texts along with the language represented by them should not be confined under the limits of centuries presumtuously inferred by the historians. In this respect, the historians are very short-sighted. The 'centuries' make their eyes blink as if from the strong sunlight and milleniums almost blur their vision.

4320 dha dhe gra ṣa-gha (bright bright sun be-fut.
= Very bright sun will be there.

This may refer to the weather-forecast system in that urban society.

The first three syllables seem to have contracted as dadhikrā in the RV, which often refers to the rolling ball of the morning sun. The whole clause means to say: The sun will be very hot.

The first three syllables dha dhe gra of this text seems to reflect in Hindi dhadhak nf. (the flame of the fire), dhadhak-nā (verb). The first syllable dha also occurs alone, where it is either a verb or a noun. It has appeared in due course that, at the isolating stage of Indus, an object was indicated by its verbal idea. That is to say, the sun was indicated as '(it) shines', which soon turned into the noun. Its reduplicated form dha dhe perhaps means '(it) shines brightly', and soon later it became an adjective, qualifying the following gra (moving fire =) 'sun', meaning 'very bright sun'. The full text probably also means: very bright sun will appear.

Its Vedic form dadhi (deaspirated at the first syllable) originally meant 'very bright', which, instead of referring to sun, somehow signified 'curd', perhaps on account of its whiteness in the pastoral Vedic Society.

The same dadhi-appears in the older dadhy-añc (later dadhī-ca, -ci) which Roth connects with dadhikrā. Perhaps dadhyañc refers to the bending of the sun through its course in the sky from sun-rise to sun-set. Should we suppose that dadhyañc or dadhikrā was originally the sun-god, variously modified in meaning later on? Dadhīca's lending of his body for Indra's use reflects in Indra's relation with the sun.

In a recent article 'Murukan in the Indus script' (Journal the Institute of Asian Studies, March 1999), Mahadevan calls the sign 'a seated skeletal figure', which he later rightly identifies with an 'emaciated ascetic'. He further refers to the mythology relating to Dadhyañc, Dadhīca and Dadhīci. The latter nomenclature of the sign, with special reference to the ancient seer, nearly identifies the sign with the phoneme dha, originally being a word for the 'sun' at the isolating stage, then shifting for a 'horse' and also 'bow' on account of its bow-like course in the sky. At the agglutinative stage, it was reduplicated, having as distant a meaning as 'curd' on account of whiteness, but the meaning 'bow' strongly reflects in Dadhyañc and the mythology related with him. The same mythology is responsible for dha being represented by a bow D in the Brahma script. The same symbol for dha was used for the unaspirate da by turning the bow-string apart.

But Mahadevan suddenly turns to the Dravidian murukan, leaving the phonemic value of the Indus sign in lurch. We see how a preconceived notion may detract one from the real path.

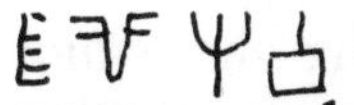

4161 va ṇa ṣa-gha

This is the future version of the isolating clause va ṇa ṣa, and may mean: from the water life will come. If the first two syllables make a phrase (the life from the water) and then a lexical word (plant), the meaning may be: the plant will grow.

When the future affix gha preceded the verb, va ṇa gha-ṣa contracted as var kṣa, then vra-kṣa, and was weakened as vṛkṣa (tree). Thus there is an intimate phonetic and semantic relation between vana and vṛkṣa.

In the colloquial Hindi, this clause has contracted with gaṣu = gaccha as gāchh-brichh (trees in general).

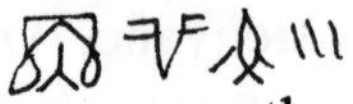

8041 ta na ṣa-ṭha (womb gem produce-past)
= The womb produced gems.

The present tense version ta na ṣa is easily comprehensible through the Vedic fossil tánas (child). But just its past version does not give a good sense.

Before taking the past affix, tana became a phrase (a gem from the womb) and then a lexical word (a child), so that the simple meaning of the clause may be: a child was born. But this too is not enough. We have to go to the background of this statement. Perhaps it was a much desired and long-awaited incident. There was a thirst for it. That is why, this whole clause in the past tense has evolved as 'thirst' in Enlish.

By this we can imagine the original home of the English people.

Once this clause is followed by ra gha (4164), the verb ra (speed) with the future affix gha, which has obliged the clause ta na sa to turn into a phrase (a gem coming from the womb of a women). Now this phrase is the subject of the verb, which slightly changes in meaning: the gem coming from the womb of a woman will go on increasing. The idea behind this new sentence is that 'the offspring will cause the family to expand'. That is to say, the phrase too is gradually contracting as lexical word.

Just as an unattested clause *va na gha ṣa has emerged as the vocable vṛkṣa in Sanskrit, we expect the obscure vocable tṛkṣa to have developed from some *ta na gha ṣa (a child will be born).

It appears that the Indus inscriptions as a whole do not represent only the isolating stage of the language, but the clauses had already begun contracting to phrases, which gradually pointed to some lexical idea. The chronological dimension of the inscriptions is as vast as the geographical.

ṣa ra ṣa gha, etc.

The extension of the clause ṣa ra ṣa by the future affix gha changes ṣa ra into a phrase: flowing from the mountain. Then this whole clause means: (the waters) flowing from the mountain will stop. This clause is often also followed by some instruction in the second line.

Thus ṣa ra ṣa gha, ra ga means: the waters flowing from the mountains will stop; make haste. But va ga in the second line gives some specific instruction. Perhaps it advises to make some reservoir (va = dwelling) of waters. Though the Indus civilisation was urban, it was strongly backed by agriculture. Even now in the countryside the waters from the reservoirs are carried to distant fields through small channels. The instrument for siphoning is now called ḍhos, which is the clause ḍho ṣa (through the instrucment siphon out) elsewhere in the Indus texts.

There are two three-line texts. The first text (4591) has na in the first line and ya ga in the third line. Thus na, ṣa-ra ṣa-gha, ya ga means: from the sky (na) the rain-water (ṣa-ra) will fall (ṣa-gha); collect. Even now in Rajasthan the rain waters are stored in well and ponds for the dry season.

The second text (4581) has ya in the first line. If it means 'sacrifice', the text seems to say: through sacrifice there will be rain-fall; do sacrifice. This reflects in Gita (3,14): yajñād bhavati parjanyaḥ.

Once the main text is preceded by what one can doubtfully read brya yo (water-fire-wind comfort) which seems to say: the rain-fall gives comfort.

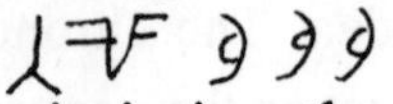

4283 ni ni ni ṣa-ṭha (heaven pl. be-past)
= There were many heavens.

If the three ni specify the number 'three' itself, it seems to reflect in a Vedic passage (RV. 1, 35, 6), which too is more or less enigmatic: there are three heavens; two (of them) are the laps of Savitṛ; one is in the world of yama, subduing men.

As a rule, however, three syllables just show plurality. As long as the words were monosyllabic, the plurality was shown through repetition. But when the bisyllabic words emerged in the language, -ṣa was added to show it.The transition to the next stage was gradual. In respect of the verb the language was agglutinative, but in respect of substantive it was still isolating.

In the RV (7, 103, 7c) the contracted form ṣ-ṭha of the agglutinative form ṣa-ṭha (be-past) has been used with pari (around): pari ṣ-ṭha (around be-past) = (You have) surrounded (the pond).

This form has been understood neither by the editors of the pada-text nor by Sāyaṇa, Roth, Macdonell and Geldner, because it has been physically lifted from the agglutinative Indus. It is not the Vedic form from sthā.

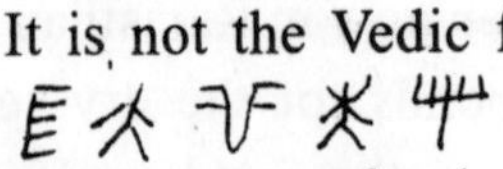

4325 ta gra ṣa ra-gha (god sun brilliance fire-fut.
= Of the god sun the brilliance will shine.

The last syllable shows that ra-gha is a future form meaning 'will shine'. The syllable ṣa is the subject meaning 'brilliance'. Then gra may be the 'prossessor' sun, qualified by ta (divine). The text means: Of the divine sun the brilliance will shine.

At the agglutinative stage, when the verb merged with subject qualifying it, the shining brilliance of the divine sun (ta gra ṣa ra) needed some new verb. The fate of the phrase is later not known.

At the inflexional stage, in the RV. 3, 62, 10 we find the same phrase paraphrased anew with a filler verb "dhīmahi" (we would receive): ta (devasya) gra (savitur) ṣa (vareṇyam) ra (bhargaḥ) dhīmahi. In the Vedic stanza, tat was imported to begin the first verse, and devasya was put in the second verse:

tat (—) savitur (gra) vareṇyaṃ (ṣa)
bhargo (ra) devasya (ta) dhīmahi.

"We would receive that excellent light of the divine sun (which should inspire our thought)".

ca na ṣa ra 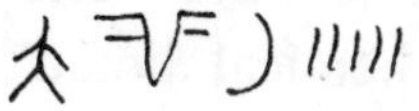

Now, when the meaning of ca na ṣa is somewhat clear, which is distinct from ca ṇa ṣa the isolated text ca na ṣa ra may be examined semantically.

The last syllable ra is probably the pluperfect affix. Then ṣa (embryo) is the verb with na (pearl) as the subject. With reference to na (pearl), ca may be conceived to mean 'oyster'. Then perhaps the whole text means: from the oyster the pearl used to be cultivated.

This should have been the flourishing business of that

ancient community and should have been the edict of the shops dealing with gems and preceious stones.

The meaning too, then, may be slightly modified: The pure cultivated pearls (sold here).

The text around Paśupati

ru i yū ṣi na ṣa ra 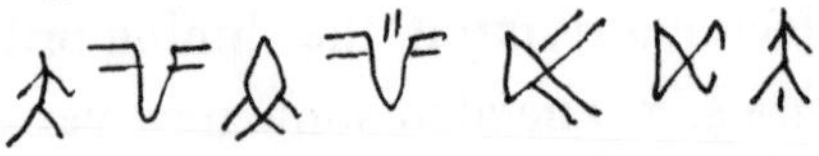

The text is a little obsure graphically on the third syllable from the right. Its ordinary form  is probably ya, but this form, if read with the following ṣi, seems to reflect in the Vedic yūs 'soup, sauce, broth' (Latin jus). Just provisionally we may read the 3rd and 4th together as yū ṣi. The last syllable seems to make a pluperfect form with ṣa, meaning 'had produced, used to produce'. Then na preceding this pluperfect form may be its subject, the preceding phrase yū ṣi being the oblique case. Thus "from yū ṣi gems used to be produced" may be the possible meaning. The semantic problem centres round yū ṣi.

Because gems are said to have been produced from yū ṣi, it is probably a 'chemical liquid'. The first two syllables, ru (fire) i (movement), qualifying yū ṣi, perhaps means 'put-on-fire, decocted, fermented'. Thus "the decocted chemical liquid used to produce gems" may be the possible meaning.

The memory of this chemical process seems to reflect in the RV (1, 1, 3): agninā rayim aśnavat (through Agni one may get wealth), though it itself seems to be the paraphrasing of another Indus text  ra na ṣa (fire gem embryo) = the fire generates (artificial) gems (through some chemical process).

We see how the transformation of the devastated urban culture into the pastoral culture is so smooth. Just some change in the warfare technology in the medieval Indian history drastically deteriorated the social status of some professionally warrior clans who are now rated as backward communities, destined to lower professions.

The Longest Indus Text

1623

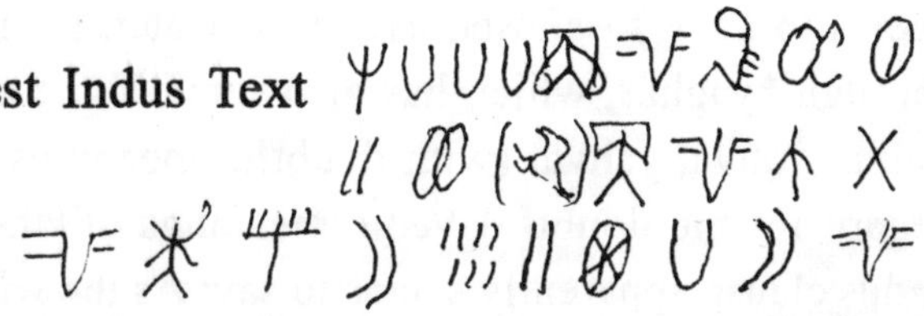

An attempt had been made earlier (from Indus to Sanskrit, Pt. III, pp. 88-90) to understand this text. Neither the reading nor the interpretation was satisfactory. Now, with more information about the Indus language and more knowledge about the urbanised state of the Indus society, we may try it again.

It is almost certain that ṣa ṭha in the middle of the first line is a past form (be-past = there was). Its contracted form ṣ-ṭha once occurs in the RV (7, 103, 7c). Its later reduction to *s-ta is unattested, but its finally fossilised form thā is available in Hindi. Though the first sign of the first line is uncertain, we may read it lu, which, with the following bha, at least reflects in the Sanskrit root lubh (1. to go astray 2. to long for 3. to allure). The first five signs read: lu bha dhe ṣa-ṭha. The syllable dhe (light) preceding the verb ṣa-ṭha (there was) is the subject, and bha (sky) preceding it is the oblique case, qualified by lu, which as imagined from rubheti (fog, steam) of the lexicon, should mean 'foggy'. The meaning 'to go astray' of lubh should reflect in 'fog'. Thus a workable meaning may be the following: In the foggy sky, there was light.

The following clause, ga (star) Pl. + ṇa (to shine) seems to be conceptually connected with it through the conjunction "because": In the foggy sky there was light, because the stars shone.

In the second line the first clause terminates at the third syllable. The first clause ya (wind) gha (sound) ṣu (embryo) seems to have fossilesed as yahas (water, strenght, power) through *yaghas, which has also some Vedic cognates like yahu, yahva, yahvat (with doubtful meanings). Having no regard for the doubtful Vedic meanings of the fossil, the Indus clause apparently seems to say: As the wind produced a rattling sound....It is naturally connected with the following clause. The first sign of the following clause probably reads b-ra (ba 'water' + ra 'fire') meaning the 'lightning-cloud'. On the basis of a wornout and decayed vocable bṛsī (the roll of the twisted grass), the bird-sign may be read sī, and the possible accent on it has reduced bra to bṛ. The clause bra sī seems to mean: the lightning-cloud flew (because sa = bird). But here perhaps bra sī is a phrase: the flying lightning-cloud. The final syllable ra (speed) is the verb and the preceding cha (unsteady) is an adverb. Now, bra sī cha ra = the flying lightning cloud moved unsteadily.

The last line is not difficult to read. The third syllable ga may be an injunctive affix after the verb ṇa (to know). Then ṣu ṇa-ga = Know the truth. The following ci ra (time speed) and dha na (sound knowledge) would have been little clauses at the isolating stage: ci ra = the time passed, dha na = the sound was known. The former is attested through ciram, etc. in Sanskrit. But, because cerebrals have gradually been replaced by the dentals in Vedic, the fossils of dha na may be sought in the dental transformations. Fortunately, dhan 'to sound' is there in Sanskrit Colloquially also, ḍhan-

ḍhan refers to sound. In this text, both ci ra and dha na are probably phrases. Thus, ci ra = for a long time, and dha na = as made known, reported. The last clause ta gra ṣa means: the brilliant sun shone = the sun shone brilliantly. The whole line may be put thus: Know it well: for a long time, reportadly, the sun shone brilliantly.

Now the whole stanza may be put together in a coherent way: In the foggy sky there was light, because the stars were shining. As the wind made a rattling sound, the lightning-cloud flying (around) moved unsteadily. Know it well: for a long time, as it is reported, the sun was shining brilliantly. (This was an evil omen).

The transcription of the text:

lu bha dhe ṣa-ṭha, ga ga ga ṇa
ya gha ṣu, bra sī cha ra
ṣu ṇa ga, ci ra, dha na, ta gra ṣa

The next perhaps reports the situation preceding some tragic event. We know that the Indus culture was not only urban but also highly technically advanced, as much as to invite natural calamities due to disturbance in the equilibrium of the nature. The Indus culture did not collapse all of a sudden. The nature had been giving warnings through minor events which remained unnoticed.

2527 la ḍha gha 

There is no doubt about the reading of the text. It is a clause, gha being either the future affix or just for emphasis. Let us concentrate on la dha and search for its shadow in the later phase of the language.

There is the possibility of la undergoing rhotacism, and of ḍha being dentalised. Then we suppose that la ḍha transited into the Vedic language as *ṛdha through *ra dha. There is a verb ṛdh 'to increase' in Vedic.

The syllable la is semantically connected with 'time', and ḍha meaning 'drum' may refer to some area of light in the empty space, later identified with the heaven. Now, the syllablic group la ḍha (time space) seems to say: the time expands.

With the affix gha, the whole clause seems to have fossilised as ṛdhak in Vedic. Then the clause la ḍha gha probably says: the (concept of) time indeed encompasses (the whole universe). That is to say, the time is as expansive as the space. Briefly, this clause asserts ' the identity of time and space'.*)

Though the word kāla was later restricted to 'time' alone, originally it stood for 'space and time'. The compound dik-kāla later restored the original duality.

ci h̲a śa nu ṣa, va ga 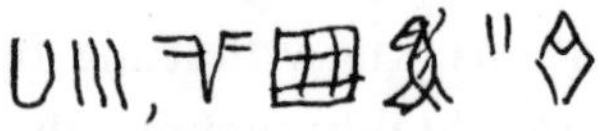

The central part of the text, namely śa nu ṣa, draws our attention. Its fossilised form in Vedic may be *śanus, but it is unattested. Its further fossilisation may come to *śarus, which too is unattested. But its shorter form śaru f. is said to mean 'spear, arrow'. If this meaning reflects in the Indus text, śaru may be confirmed as the fossilised form of the Indus clause śa nu ṣa.

In the traditional Sanskrit lexicons of the monosyllabic words, śa (being the first syllable of śastra 'weapon') means

---

*) The original meaning of the Vedic verb ṛdh may be 'to go beyond time and space', 'to excel'. The adverb ṛdhak originally means 'away' as judged from its association with kṛ (to put away) and contrast with iha (here, in own house: away). cf. the relevant Vedic passages.

'weapon'. The next syllable nu suggests some concrete object, probably 'body'. Perhaps 'the weapon harms the body' may be the intended meaning. It is in this context that the first phrase ci ha (trully speaking) and the last clause va ga (please guard yourself) have some relevance.

Though the root śṛ is there in the Vedic language to derive śara, śaru, etc., it has really been deduced from these words. In a number of cases, the arrow of derivation has to be changed to be more scientific in etymology.

la śa ṣa, ya ga 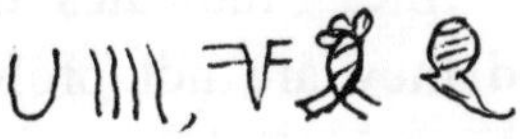

The reading of this text is doubtless. The first syllable la, represented by the hind-leg of an animal, has actually been identified through a rustic Hindi word lathār (the strike by the hind-leg), which is really a prehistoric word, either a phrase of the agglutinative Indus or a clasue of the isolating Indus. The syllable la here means either just the hind-leg or a similar injurious object or the animal itself. The second syllable śa means 'injury', which is the inherent sense of this syllable in many other words. Thus this clause seems to mean: the hind-leg (of an animal) causes injury; do take care. Probably lathār also had a similar meaning at the isolating stage.

Later, the first syllable seems to have undergone rhotacism and, due to accent on the following ṣ́a at the inflexional stage, it should have been reduced to ṛ. The resulting word ṛśa occurs in AV 4, 4, 7 and the extended ṛśya in RV 8, 4, 10 and VS 24, 27, 37 meaning 'the goat-antelope' (popularly known as ban-bakrā).

The context of this text appears to be 'hunting', and the hunter is supposed to have been warned against the strike by the hind-leg of this animal, although the horns of the goat-antelope are more harmful. Then, probably, the clause la śa ṣa means: the goat-antelope causes harm or injury. Supposedly, all harmful creatures were indicated by la.

2519 ra ca va u, na ka ṣa ṭha

The reading of the text is probably correct. The text written in two lines indicates that there are two groups of ideas, and they are not probably syntactically related.

In the first line, if ra = fire and va = water, the next syllable in each case may be the corresponding verb, namely: ca = to burn and u = to cool. Thus ra ca va u = the fire burns ; the water cools.

In the second line, the last two syllables ṣa-ṭha indicate the verb in the past tense. Then ka preceding the verb is the subject and na preceding the latter is the oblique case. Thus na ka ṣa-ṭha = in the sky the light appeared.

By the time of the Vedic language, when ṭha was dentalised and deaspirated, -s-, coming between two stops, was lost, and there was nakta (for *naksta) 'night', literally 'the bright one'. In other dialects, s, while going, aspirated the preceding k.

It also appears that ṭha (past) is connected with each clause: the fire burn-past, the water cool-past, and in the sky the light embryo-past. It is difficult to evaluate the presence of the past tense in these clsuses. It appears that not only the past but all the tense-affixes were originally just emphatic. There could be only shades of difference in their meanings: the fire just burns, the water just cools and the sky is just bright. But how ṭha was restricted to past, ha to perfect, ra to pluperfect, gha to future, and ga to injunction (as far as known) relates to the psychology of the language.

In the following text, the last three syllables too appear to make the Vedic vocable nakta:

4073 ci ha, ta na ka ṭha

But ci ha (truly speaking) kept apart, the following syllable ta then becomes reducndant. Therefore, probably ta (womb) na (gem) make another phrase 'a gem in the womb', referring to the future child, which may be the subject of this clause. The meaning perhaps is: the gem in the womb (of a woman) is indeed a joy or bliss. The syllable ṭha is here the emphatic "be".

The Veterinary Hospital

Graphically, the sign 394 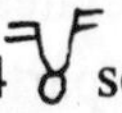 seems to be the combination of 342 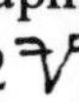 ṣa and 374 ṭa and the two texts, where it occurs, are the following:

2318 na ṣṭa gha 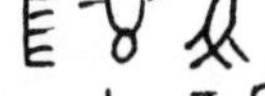
1394 ṣṭa ra pa 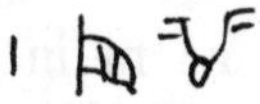

The future form 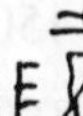 ṣṭha-gha (stay-future) has fossilised as a new verb sthag (to stop) in Sanskrit. Even some past participles of Sanskrit have developed as new verbs in Apabhraṃśa; e.g. upa-viṣṭa (seated, sitting) has become baiṭha- (to sit), pra-viṣṭa (entered) has become paiṭṭha- (to enter), and so on. In Hindi, they are bäṭh-, päṭh-, etc. In the same way, ṣṭa-gha above could have fossilised as stak (pratighāte) 'to repulse' in Sansk. (Dhatup. 19, 20). Then "na-repulse-future" means something like this: the gem will be repulsed. If we take a rustic word naṭṭhā (from na-ṣṭa) into account, said about a milch cattle remaining barren even after mating the male, na ṣṭa gha certainly means as above, indicating that the animal has not been able to conceive. In popular parlance, the 'animal seed' is called maṇi (gem).

The clause ṣṭa ra pa should have theoretically fossilised as *starp, but only star (stṛ) 'to strew, spread' is attested in Sanskrit. The syllable pa at the end does not appear to have formed an intimate part of the clause. Then ṣṭa ra is the main clause, a pluperfect form like ca-ra (be-pluperfect = had been). Perhaps ṣṭa ra means 'had been repulsed', pa being the object. If the two texts express the same idea, it says: the gem had been repulsed, that is, the milch cattle has not been able to conceive.

Clearly, the statement relates to the animal husbandry and would have formed a part of the inscriptions near a veterinary hospital.

The surface waters

The clause 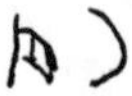 na ra in the first line is followed by 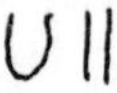 ra-ga (5410), 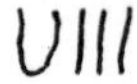 va-ga (4502) and 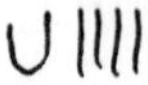 ya-ga (5418) in three texts. The reading is as much doubtless as the interpretation is uncertain.

The three injunctions expressed by ga with respect to ra (speed), va (water) and ya (action) perhaps refers to appropriate activity at right opportunity. In this connection, the first line becomes meaningful only when it relates to some natural phenomena. That is to say, some natural event is advised to be advantageously utilised at appropriate moment.

The contents of the second line, namely ra-ga (do hurry), va-ga (do irrigate) and ya-ga (do take action) suggest that na means 'river', (which is also the first syllable of na-da 'flows (and) makes noise' and ra means 'flows'. That is to say, na ra = the river flows, has begun flowing.

That technically advanced urban society, supported by agriculture, exhorts the people to make use of the flow of water in summer when the snow melts on the Himalayas. That ancient society was not foolish like ours which suffers from flood in the rainy season and from shortage of water in summer. Thus the texts appear to say:

The River has begun flowing, na ra, 

1. Do hurry (and store waters) ra ga 

2. Do irrigate (the thirsty lands) va ga 

3. Do take proper action (to utilise waters)  ya ga

The Indus clause na ra (the river flows) has now fossilised as nal (pipe), nālā (small canal) in certain dialects.

(B-a)

The solitary Indus signs

The Indus ligature ṣ-ṭha is obviously a combination of ṣa and ṭha, which occurs, once as a subject + verb (ṣa ṭha) and several times elsewhere as the verb 'to be' + the past affix ṭha (ṣa-ṭha) in longer clauses. If the ligature ṣ-ṭha is the prehistoric form of the Vedic verb sthā (to stand), ṣṭhā in the Dhātupāṭha, the traditional grammarians may be supposed to know the meanings of its constituents ṣa and ṭha when they mean gatinivṛtti (cessation of movement) by it.

When a present or future tense is expressed, there is also some subject: ta ṣṭha (gha). When the subject is preceded by a syllable, it may be the oblique case: na bha ṣṭha (gha). Sometimes the oblique case + the subject become a phrase, because they contract with the verb to form a new vocable: śa ma ṣṭha (gha) has become śaṃ-stha (happiness). The Vedic verb sthag (to stop) appears to be the contracted form of the verb ṣṭha gha (stop-future).

The presence of the verb ṣṭha in isolation sparks a very modern idea about its use. It is a signal of some kind. We are somehow aware of the fact that the Indus was an urban civilisation which could use devices of the advanced society. Thus all the solitary signs in the inscriptions are signals:

Perhaps, ṣṭha stands for 'stop' in respect of the vehicular control; ṭha (circle, disc) stands for 'turn' (to the left or to the right); ra (speed) for 'go on'*; na for 'no'; ni for 'in', and so on. Some syllables appear to give warnings against the future events: dra 'hot sun' (ahead), pra 'storm', etc. Even some bisyllabic texts may stand for such instructions.

The presence of the animal figures in the texts indicates the various signs of dangers and warnings conceived through the mind of those primitive people.

---

* Even now, some walking human figure on the cross-road allows a pedestrian to walk across the road.

Though it is clear that each solitary sign is a signal of some kind, we can form some idea about the following additional signs only:

tra  : help: help:
hau  : stop: (to an animal)
ka  : water (available here)
ta  : yes:
ṭha  : turn :
jha  : attention:
cū  : silence:

The following solitary signs need an x-ray examination from the point of view of their meanings:

dha 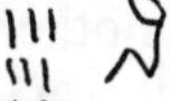
ha 
ṭa 
ca 
pha 
bha 
? yu 
yo 
ṇa 
gha 
ḍa 

Bisyllabic ṣa-clauses

As we go along the concordance of the Indus texts, noting the bisyllabic clauses ending with ṣa, we find that just a few syllables are left out in forming the pairs; e.g.

1093 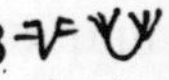 ka ṣa
7214 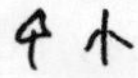 gha ṣa
1904 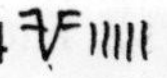 5266 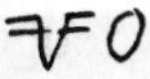 ca ṣa

1252 jha ṣa

2602 2269 ṇa ṣa

1197 da ṣa

1129 6236 dha ṣa

pa ṣa

1247 bha ṣa

1254 ma ṣa

1430 2516 la ṣa

2026 ha ṣa

The syllables which are missing at the first position are mostly those which are rare or unrepresented in the texts.

Besides, there are other consonants with other vowels at the first position; e.g. ṭho ṣa, ḍho ṣa, yo ṣa, ṇā ṣa, dheṣa, etc.

As the language transited from the isolating to the agglutinative stage, the clauses became phrases with the same body of the syllables. But at the inflexional stage, when the first syllable bore the accent the final syllable lost the vowel a. Otherwise, the clause remained intact.

Of the possible lexemes at the inflexional stage, namely kas, ghas, cas, nas, das, dhas, pas, mas, las, etc., at least puro=dhas (priest) and candra-mas (moon) are attested, riśādas already in the RV. But this last one is obscure not only to the editors of the pada-text but also to the scholars from Sāyaṇa to Geldner. The word uśanas (a mythical seer) is obscure already to the singers of the RV, not analysed in the pada-text, generally coneived as uśan, uśanā and uśana.

The Vedic mās (month) may represent the unquotable mā ṣa (the time is known), while nās in a-nās may be derived from the quotable ṇā ṣa (the knowledge grows). The clauses ṭho ṣa, ḍho ṣa, jha ṣa have not suffered any reduction due to accent on the last syllable.

From the point of view of the Vedic etymology, dhas in purodhas is connected with dhā, which also seems to be confirmed by puro-hita (priest). Geldner, RV 1,1,1 ardently advocates the identity of puro-hita and puro-dhas. But we think that this connection is unfounded. Actually, -dhas in puro-dhas is the reduced from of the clause dha ṣa (the sun is shining). Through the phrase 'the shining sun' it was restricted to just 'shining' at the inflexional stage. Thus puro-dhas means: shining in the front. It has been forcibly made identical with puro-hita lit. put in the front (qualifying Agni). Cf. -das and -mas specifically for riśādas and candra-mas.

The shorter forms uśan, uśana and uśanā of uśanas have been conceived as connected with vaś (to wish), but really -nas seems to have been added to *uśa-.

Beyond the Texts

The affixes which are not attested in the inscription are the following:

1. The prefix ā- for past
ā-ṣa (past-be) = (there) was
ā-ha (past-say) = said
2. The suffix - ha for perfect (present perfect)
ma-ha (time-perfect) = has grown old
3. The suffix - ra for pluperfect (past perfect)
ca-ra (be-pluperfect) = had been
4. The suffix - ma for past
sa-ma (be-past)

It was later contracted to s-ma. In Sanskrit it turns a present form into past: gacchati (goes): gacchati sma (went).

Some clauses reconstructed on their basis may be the following:

a. i-ti ha ā-ṣa (thus say past-be)
= Thus, they say, it was

This clause was naturalised in Sanskrit as the following:

iti ha āsa

Later it contracted as a lexical word: itihāsa (story)

b. tata ma-ha (father time-perfect)
= the father has grown old

c. nana ma-ha (mother time-perfect)
= The mother has grown old.

In the RV these two clauses contracted as tatā-maha and

nanā-mahī (grandmother). On their analogy, later, even pitā-maha and mātā-maha (with their fem. forms in -mahī) came into being.

The agglutinative Indus was left so much far behind that even Pāṇini could not detect -maha as a perfect form from the monosyllabic verb ma (time) 'to grow old'.

There is no clause imaginable with cara which, by the time of Pāṇini, was not more than a secondary suffix in the sense of ex-, former (bhūta-pūrva) P. 5,3,53.

But the following vocables are the contracted forms of the clauses at the agglutinative stage:

kucara = ku cara (on the earth had been)

gocara = go cara (in view had been)

Perhaps cara also meant 'had stolen away', which combined with its object paṭa (cloth), and paṭaccara (thief) became a word of abuse.

Probably -cara is not the only obsolete pluperfect form used in Sanskrit. Even dāra (wife), māra (cupid), jāra (paramour), etc. are obsolete pluperfect forms turning up as nouns in Sanskrit. Even cora (thief) may be a primitive pluperfect form (= had stolen away).

The Oblique cases

For the oblique cases, there was, in the beginning, only -ti, and only the following form is attested:

i-ti (this-oblique case) = thus

Later, the possessive suffix -sa (in śa-sa 'long-eared', assimilated as śaśa 'hare' cf. Latin caso) was extended by -ya. But there is no quotable example in the prehistoric form of Sanskrit. First of all, it appeared in the pronominal forms (ka-sya, ta-sya, etc.), and -s- became the distinctive features of the pronominal endings.

The affix for the object was -ma:

ṇara-ma

gāva-ma

The plural forms

Now we are dealing with the agglutinative stage of Indus which are not recorded in any inscriptions. The texts which may appear are only reconstructed.

Both in declension and conjugation, the pl. affix was ṣa, which is nowhere to be seen in the extant Indus inscriptions. We just imagine that the clause ṇa ra (an animal is going) became a phrase (a going animal) and then a lexical word (a man). Similarly, gā va (goes into the pen) became a lexical word gāva (a cow). Their plural forms are:

ṇara-ṣa

gāva-ṣa

Even the verbs made plural forms in the same way, but the sg. base slightly turned towards u-:

ā-sa ā-ṣu-ṣa

ā-ha ā-hu-ṣa

Because ṣa is at the head of the three sibilants (ṣa sa śa) in the Indus syllabary, it was conceived to be the plural affix.

The clauses with the plural form would have been the following:

gāvaṣa āṣuṣa = The cows were there.

ṇaraṣa āhuṣa = People said.

It is interesting to note that the plural forms were monotonous till the last days of the agglutinative Indus.

The Dual forms

Perhaps there was also -ha to show duality of the subject and object:

ṇara ṇara-ha
gāva gāva-ha

The same -ha would have been added to i- and u- bases:

kavi kavi-ha
ripu ripu-ha

Because there are two ha in the Indus syllabary, it was supposed to represent 'two'. Gradually, it turned up as the dual affix.

Transition

Though we can reconstruct a few more clauses, we stop here. Now it is worthwhile to show the transit of some of the agglutinative forms into the inflexional Vedic language.

With the forms like ṇarasa, gāvasa, ṇaraha, gāvaha, kaviha, ripuha in declension, and āsa āsusa āha āhusa in conjugation, the agglutinative Indus stood on the threshold of the inflexional stage.

Here, due to accent on the first syllable, the final a was lost:

ṇaraṣa	náras
gāvaṣa	gā́vas
āṣa	ās
āṣuṣa	āsus
āha	āh
āhuṣa	āhus
ṇaraha	nárah
gāvaha	gāvah

kaviha kávih
ripuha ripuh

At this stage, the -as part in declension and -us part in conjugation were taken to be the pl. endings. The analysis of náras as nar-as and of gā́vas as gāv-as highlighted the base nar- and gāu- on the cut-point, giving rise to some vowel-sandhi rules. On the basis of -as for pl., -s was conceived to be the sg. ending. Later, in the Vedic language, gāu- was reduced to gau- in the weak cases, and nar- too was reduced to nṛ- only before the consonantal endings: gav-ā gau-bhis, but nar-ā nṛ-bhis.

In the conjugational forms, the sg. āsa was reduced ās, and that is fortunately attested in the RV (10, 129, 3c), but in the RV itself this reduced form was expanded in various persons and numbers as follows:

3. - ās-an
2. - ās-ta
1. ās-am ās-ma

In 3p and 2p an -ī- was interposed between the base and the endings: 3. ās-ī-t 2. ās-ī-s.

But these forms were analysed differently by the Vedic grammarians:

3. ā-as-ī-t ā-s-an
2. ā-as-ī-s ā-s-ta
1. ā-as-am ā-s-ma

This analysis gave birth to the unexpected verb as 'to be' in the language, and with this verb the Aryans migrated to west Asia and Europe, twisting as to es (lat. es-ti). Even the weak base s started from here (Ved. s-anti lat. sunt).

From the forms āha and āhus, Pāṇini concived the verb ah. The reduced form āh became āḥ in vedic and was used as a word for 'grief'.

Although the root as continued in the present system in the Vedic, ah did not go beyond five forms (also having present sense).

The dual forms tell us wonderful stories.

From narah and gāvah, the final h disappeared after lengthening the preceding vowel:

narā gāvā

Similarly,

kavī ripū

When the vowel-sandhi began to operate in the Vedic language, the final h in kavi-ha and ripu-ha initially vetoed its operation, but later even when it disappeared, its memory made the final ī ū uncontractable.

The laryngeal H of the modern Indoeuropeanists is not totally fictitious.

Later the dual ā was also extended by -u (narau gāvau), and -au became the regular dual ending.

Of the oblique affix -ti in i-ti, only -t has been left in abl. sg. devāt, though iti itself has survived as a particle. The affix -ma was reduced to -m at the inflexional stage.

The later phase of the Indus language is what we call the Vedic language.